ORLANDO

BY

JONATHAN CARLISLE

razOr
bill

Orlando

RAZORBILL
Published by Penguin Group
Penguin Young Readers Group
345 Hudson Street, New York, New York 10014, U.S.A.
Penguin Books Ltd, 80 Strand, London WC2R 0RL, England
Penguin Books Australia Ltd, 250 Camberwell Road,
Camberwell, Victoria, 3124 Australia
Penguin Books Canada Ltd, 10 Alcorn Avenue,
Toronto, Ontario, Canada M4V 3B2
Penguin Books (NZ) cnr Airborne and Rosedale Roads,
Albany, Auckland 1310, New Zealand

Penguin Books Ltd, Registered Offices:
Harmondsworth, Middlesex, England

1 3 5 7 9 10 8 6 4 2

Library of Congress Cataloging-in-Publication Data
is available

Printed in the United States of America

Contents

INTRODUCTION

One perfect nose and a pair of soulful brown eyes to rule them all . . .

While *Lord of the Rings* fanatics worldwide have been in a frenzy these past few years, watching their favorite story unfold at the local movie theater, many equally breathless fans have been rushing to the cineplex as well—to see these same films for an altogether different reason.

Orlando Bloom.

With a face that could melt a million hearts, Orlando has taken both Hollywood and the moviegoing public by storm. His combination of gorgeous looks and blazing talent has made him the hottest performer in Tinseltown, appealing to fans and casting directors alike. Which makes it no surprise that his career has taken a meteoric path.

Most actors spend years perfecting their skills, performing in dozens of smaller films and TV shows before getting their big break. But Orlando's good looks and acting chops propelled him to the top of the profession—all before he had finished his education.

In spite of his incredibly fast rise to fame, Orlando's powerful portrayals in *The Lord of the Rings, Black Hawk Down,* and *Pirates of the Caribbean* have proven to the world what *Rings* director Peter Jackson instinctively knew—and what millions of Orlando's loving fans would happily scream to the world if they could:

Orlando Bloom is the real deal.

Orlando realized early on that acting was in his blood. He studied hard to gain the skills that allowed him to endure the grueling 18-month *Rings* shoot. (His daredevil ways—resulting in numerous broken bones over the years—didn't hurt in toughening him up for the experience, either.)

Yes, Orlando Bloom *is* gorgeous and talented, but like many of the characters he portrays, he is brave and strong as well.

But you already know how great Orlando is. Now let's look at how he got that way—the hard work, the dedication, the shocking secret that upended everything he thought he knew about his family, and the tragedy that came close to not only ending his career, but also his very life.

CHAPTER ONE
THE SEEDS OF STARDOM

One day Orlando Bloom was a cute English kid reciting poetry to his neighbors. The next, it seemed, he was floating through Disneyland, standing next to his favorite actor and the hottest producer in Hollywood while thousands of fans screamed his name.

It didn't actually happen that quickly, of course. In between, there were years of study and sweat. But Orlando Bloom's rise to fame *was* quicker than most. So quick that some say Orlando is blessed with a special kind of luck.

But is Orlando just lucky? Or is his success a result of the fact that he embodies so many traits that elevate him above the rest—like his dashing, leading-man looks or his seemingly effortless ability to make every character he inhabits noble and just?

It's tough to call.

Perhaps Orlando's fortune is just the universe's way of saying that every once in a while, a good guy gets to win. While Orlando Bloom has become a star and an idol and the object of so many dreams, no one can begrudge him his success. In every way, in his looks, his talent, and his temperament, there is one fact that people both in and out of Hollywood acknowledge every day:

Orlando Bloom deserves to be a star.

Orlando Bloom was born on January 13, 1977. Many fans over the years have read that Orlando was born in Kent and mistakenly thought that it was an abbreviation. They assumed that he spent his early years in Kentucky.

But make no mistake. Orlando is English, through and through. He was born in Kent, a county in England where the city of Canterbury lies.

Orlando grew up in Canterbury with his mother, Sonia, his father, Harry, his big sister, Samantha, and his cherished dog, Maude. The Bloom family was known for possessing great intelligence and a great love of culture, which is no surprise, considering the backgrounds of Orlando's parents.

Orlando's father, Harry Bloom, was a wealthy lawyer in South Africa. He was also a novelist and an anti-apartheid activist who took great personal risks to fight his government's racist practices.

Harry wrote several highly acclaimed books, including his 1956 debut novel *Transvaal Episode,* which was banned in South Africa because authorities thought the book would disturb race relations. He also wrote the book for the first ever all-African opera.

Harry spent much of his time in the fight to secure equal rights for blacks at a time when they were discriminated against in the cruelest ways. He could have used his position as a lawyer to get himself a judgeship, but he sacrificed that opportunity, choosing instead to fight against government injustice.

Harry often delivered books to anti-apartheid prisoners and did what he could to provide them with moral support. He even worked with that country's top anti-apartheid activist and future president, Nelson Mandela, whom he called a close friend. Harry was so dedicated to the cause, in fact, that he was eventually jailed for his efforts.

While Orlando's father was a brave and principled

man, his mother was a free and adventurous spirit in her own right. Sonia Copeland Bloom cherished the arts. She was in love with words (a trait that would eventually influence Orlando's decision to become an actor), and she was a firm believer in living life to the fullest.

When Sonia and Harry got together, no one could deny the fact that they made an intensely interesting couple.

As the years went on, Harry found himself ready for a quieter, more peaceful life than the one he'd built in South Africa. The Bloom family packed up their belongings and moved to England. It was there that Orlando made his entrance into the world.

There are several rumors in the press about how Orlando got his unusual name. Many think it was inspired by a novel of the same name by the legendary writer Virginia Woolf. Orlando says that this story isn't true. His mother told him he was named for a seventeenth-century composer named Orlando Gibbons. But Sonia herself revealed that the purpose of Orlando's name was really much more practical—it was easy for his father to remember.

"Harry had trouble with his students' names,"

Sonia explained, "and thought he would always remember an Orlando. The family thought Orlando might get teased, but he has always loved having that name."

Growing up, Sonia took Orlando and his sister, Samantha, to see plays as often as she could. They would go to the Marlowe Theatre in Canterbury or down to one of London's many historic stages. Sonia did her best to ensure that Orlando was exposed to influences beyond what he might see on TV and in pop culture.

"I never knew who the Spice Girls were, or anyone like that," Orlando explains.

But while he was exposed to serious culture, Orlando's mum did allow him just one guilty pleasure—trashy American television.

It was on the American TV show *Dynasty* that Orlando found his first crush—1980s soap star Linda Evans.

"I used to watch *Dynasty* as a kid," Orlando recalls wistfully. "My aunt is a commercial producer in New York, and she's done a commercial with her. I can still remember getting this signed photo of Linda. . . ."

Orlando's mother inspired not only his love of the arts, but his sense of daring as well. Throughout her life, Sonia Bloom had an adventurous streak. When she was not running her foreign-language school in England, Sonia would go off on impulsive excursions. She would ride across Mexico on a donkey or travel to Russia, where she helped that country establish its first PGA Junior Golf Championship.

The freedom and courage that both his parents treasured had a profound effect on Orlando. As he grew, Sonia's free spirit and love of adventures would combine with Harry's inherent bravery to make Orlando a thrill seeker and risk taker of the highest order.

But other aspects of his parents' personalities affected Orlando as well. His father's thoughtfulness, fearlessness, and incredible consideration of the plight of others loomed large in Orlando's life. It's no coincidence, therefore, that many of the movie characters Orlando has played have been heroic—men who stand up for goodness despite the odds. That type of person is one that Orlando has related to all his life—thanks to Harry Bloom.

Unfortunately, Orlando got to know Harry more by reputation than through personal relations. While Orlando was still an infant, Harry suffered a stroke. During this time, Sonia was assisted in Harry's care by a friend of hers named Colin Stone. Harry passed away soon after his stroke at the age of 68. Orlando was just four years old. A short time later, Colin Stone became Orlando and his sister's legal guardian.

While Orlando is very guarded when it comes to talking about his family, he is quick to express his love and admiration for Harry Bloom. "Harry was a great man," Orlando says. "It was as though he'd done his job and he left the world."

So for most of their lives, Orlando and Samantha were raised by their mom and Colin. Orlando had a happy childhood, and it was clear at an early age that he was developing into a rambunctious and fearless young boy.

"I was a little bit crazy," Orlando has said. "Not crazy-crazy, but I was always the first one to jump off the wall or dive into the lake, without really thinking about the consequences of my actions."

Thanks to this kind of daring, Orlando kicked off one of his lifelong "hobbies"—breaking bones. When he was just nine years old, he fell while skiing and broke his leg. He spent the next year in a cast.

The incredibly active Orlando was forced to

spend that time sitting at home, feeling sorry for himself, and gorging on his favorite junk foods. "I was eating biscuits and chocolate bars," Orlando says with a laugh. "I was a porker."

As he grew older, Orlando's wild-child tendencies would continue. At 15, he decided to get a tattoo—a yellow sun on the left side of his belly. "I sort of lied and told my mom, 'Oh, it's only going to last a couple of years,'" the sly Orlando confessed.

When considering an activity that was risky or adventurous, it never took much for Orlando to make the leap. But while his daredevil tendencies were a great part of his life, Orlando's artistic sense usually won out. He was encouraged to perform in his school's plays and to read at the local Kent Festival, where children would have poetry- and Bible-reading contests.

At 10 years old, Orlando would stand onstage and recite works by great poets, like Robert Frost. From the very beginning, little Orlando took audiences by storm.

These early experiences introduced Orlando to the concept of acting. It was here that he found that the craft was in his blood. "I don't know why my mom wanted my sister and me to do it,"

Orlando explained, "but it was great. I loved it. She always encouraged us to be creative. She would have people come around and teach us art and pottery and stuff like that."

Years later, after his *Lord of the Rings* success, Orlando spoke with a journalist about these contests and proceeded to recite, from memory, one of the poems he had read as a child. The poem was Robert Frost's "Stopping by Woods on a Snowy Evening." This lucky journalist gazed into Orlando's eyes as he recited the lines, summoned up from childhood memory, as fresh as if he had read it just that morning—"The woods are lovely, dark and deep / But I have promises to keep / And miles to go before I sleep," Orlando whispered, entrancing all who could hear him.

Orlando says those early performances gave him a "sensitivity to language in terms of vocalizing it."

But while he enjoyed the performing itself, as a child Orlando was a bit confused about acting. He thought that by *portraying* the wonderful heroes he saw on television and in the movies, he could literally *become* them.

"Watching these larger-than-life characters," said Orlando, "I decided I wanted to become an actor."

There was one moment in his early years when Orlando's desire to be a real-life hero was nearly overwhelming. When he was nine, there was a neighborhood girl who was Orlando's girl-friend—sort of. He and the other boys would have running races in their local park each day, and the winner would get to be this girl's boyfriend. Even at nine, Orlando had a romantic streak, a sense that he wanted to rescue the damsel in distress. To protect her. To be her hero.

So to Orlando, it seemed obvious that if he actually *was* Superman, if he was able to fly and be strong and have all the powers that his favorite superhero had, he could rescue this girl.

So Orlando pretended to be the Man of Steel and then ran his heart out to win the hand of this girl—if only for one day.

But soon Orlando made a startling discovery. As he watched plays with his mother and learned more about the world, he realized that the movie version of Superman, and the other heroes he saw in the media, weren't real—they were characters being portrayed by actors.

To Orlando, this was a revelation.

"When I was younger, I had an incredible

imagination, like most kids," Orlando recalls. "Once I was old enough to realize that those characters weren't real, that they were actors—once I realized that I could be Superman or I could be [Paul Newman's] the Hustler or I could be Daniel Day-Lewis's character in *The Last of the Mohicans*—I was like, 'Man, I can become an actor and be *all* of those things.'"

So Orlando's destiny was sealed. Both the experience of acting locally and the desire to be a larger-than-life hero on-screen drove him toward bigger and better things. His early success at the readings, his continued enjoyment of school plays, and his mother's love and encouragement of all things creative placed him on a path.

It was as if everything in Orlando's life conspired to send him toward a career in show business. But there was one stumbling block he'd have to overcome before he could even consider making a go of it.

Few people know it, but Orlando has a condition that could have stopped his acting dreams dead in their tracks. Orlando is dyslexic.

Dyslexia is a condition that makes it hard for people to translate the sounds in words into visual concepts they can understand. Therefore dyslexics have tremendous difficulty reading words, letters, or numbers on a page. The condition has absolutely no relationship to intelligence, which sometimes places very smart people in the bizarre position of explaining to others why they can't read.

Orlando isn't the only star with the condition. Tom Cruise is dyslexic as well, and got cast in roles throughout the early part of his career by ad-libbing at auditions and generally charming the casting people.

Like Tom Cruise, Orlando showed the strength and perseverance that would mark his career and struggled to make the best of a bad situation.

Orlando has said that his dyslexia made learning at school "hard graft" (which is a British way of saying it gave him a hard time). "I am dyslexic, so education was always a bit tricky," Orlando admitted. "But I got all my exams and degrees. I just had to work harder to get them."

In fact, Orlando worked as hard as he could to adjust to his condition and showed that he had the determination to overcome even the hardest of hardships. While his school marks weren't always the best, he was able to learn to read without giving up hope, and because of that, he was able to move on with his acting.

Inspired by his early successes onstage, Orlando participated more and more in plays at his school, St. Edmund's in Canterbury. Sensing his talent, his teachers would give him interesting roles, including the sergeant in the Gilbert and Sullivan opera *The Pirates of Penzance* and—believe it or not—an old man in a 1920s musical called *The Boy Friend*.

And while he pursued his love of performing with extreme dedication, Orlando was hardly one-dimensional. He also spent time with other hobbies and interests. He learned about photography and sculpture. And finally, while still a boy, Orlando Bloom developed another interest as well—he was evolving into quite the ladies' man.

Not surprisingly, kissing girls was something that Orlando took to quickly. Orlando was quite popular with the girls of Canterbury, and he began having girlfriends at a young age.

Besides his "most wanted" status at St. Edmund's, Orlando's mother's language school also introduced Orlando to many attractive young European girls.

Orlando remembers his first kiss, which happened when he was just twelve. As he recalls with embarrassment, he was pretty clueless about how to handle it.

"My first kiss was terrible," Orlando remembered. "I was twelve, and I didn't know what to do with my teeth!"

Who wants to bet that he's figured it out since then?

Now, of course, Orlando gets to kiss some of the prettiest girls in Hollywood—for a living! To Orlando, those are just some of the perks of the job.

"If someone offers me a film where I am supposed to kiss a girl, I'm all for it!" he proclaimed. "I would even work for free!"

After starring in blockbuster after blockbuster, Orlando still can't believe he gets paid for the incredibly fun work he does. But growing up, he got a taste of hard work as well. When he was 13, he took on a job as a clay trapper at a skeet-shooting range. "I set the clay disks the gentlemen would try to shoot," Orlando explained. He enjoyed being outdoors in the fresh air but found himself a bit bored by the repetitious trapping job.

It was in this same year that Orlando discovered a less-than-pleasant job was the least of his difficulties. While the family was on vacation that summer, Sonia gave Samantha and Orlando some shocking news.

She told her children that Harry Bloom, the man they had always revered as a loving, heroic father, was not actually their father at all. Their real, biological father was Colin Stone, their legal guardian.

The news sent Orlando reeling. For a 13-year-old boy to learn that the man he idolized and adored—the man he looked up to as a father—was actually not his father at all filled him with confusion.

This is one aspect of Orlando's life that he speaks very little about in public. When reporters do ask him about it, he becomes uneasy. His body sometimes tenses up, and he looks away. The news Sonia gave Orlando during that family vacation was clearly news he was unprepared for.

On the rare occasion that Orlando does try to discuss his family situation, he struggles to find the words to describe it. He has made references to "my mother's husband" or "my legal father." He seems torn with not only how he should feel about the situation, but how he should present it to others.

In the end, though, as with everything that he

does, Orlando manages to find the bright side and put his situation in a positive light.

"It's an unusual story," Orlando admits. "But then, you show me a family and I'll show you an unusual story. I was really lucky. I had two dads."

And however conflicted Orlando may have been about the surprising news, Sonia reports that Orlando's life with her and Colin was a full one.

"Orlando has a very happy background," Sonia says. "It is something he has grown up with. Orlando is not sad. He was brought up surrounded by a loving family."

But Orlando's happy home life couldn't calm the acting bug growing inside him, and soon he felt the need to take a real shot at stardom. So at the tender age of 16, Orlando left both the comfort of his family in Canterbury and the structure of school life and took off for the big city—London— to find his fortune.

CHAPTER TWO
LIVIN' LARGE IN
LONDON

While many think of Hollywood as *the* place for those seeking a life as an actor, Hollywood is really only best for those who want to be movie or TV stars.

For stage actors, London is as historic and important as a city can be.

London's rich theatrical tradition dates back to the days of William Shakespeare's Globe Theatre. The city today is still an important training ground for some of the world's finest thespians.

Orlando admits that he was young to be leaving home, but he was more than ready for the adventure ahead and the chance to prove himself in the city where some of the finest stage actors in the world learned their craft.

"I felt good about it," said Orlando. "I've always been a bit ahead of myself and I was ready to leave. I felt like London was the place to be."

As it turned out, he was right. The London theater community was quick to recognize talent, and Orlando's was acknowledged immediately. He won a scholarship to the National Youth Theatre, one of England's top companies for young actors. The NYT's alumni roster reads like a who's who of the best of British theater, including Sir Ben Kingsley, Sir Derek Jacobi, Dame Helen Mirren, Daniel Day-Lewis, Timothy Dalton, and Michael York.

Nowadays the company's brochure lists all of these major talents plus one more—Orlando Bloom.

One of Orlando's first performances was at the Tricycle Theatre in north London. His performance was so impressive that a local agent asked to represent him. From there, it seemed that getting acting jobs, usually a constant struggle for aspiring actors, was child's play for Orlando.

Early successes included a part as a self-mutilating teenager on a TV show called *Casualty* (Orlando has described it as "a cheaper version of *ER*") and another part in a show called *Midsomer Murders*. But success didn't stop him from living life like an ordinary teenager. While in London, Orlando bought his first car, a deep-green VW Golf, for about 160 quid, or 230 American dollars.

Orlando loved his car and has even said recently that he wishes he still owned it.

Adjusting to big-city life was tough for Orlando at first. While there was much to enjoy about London, the place is not always welcoming to a fresh-faced newcomer.

"I moved to London expecting to meet a whole bunch of new mates instantly," Orlando said. "But London can be such a lonely city."

Not surprisingly, though, Orlando soon made friends, and once he had mates to pal around with, he began to play as hard as he worked. He became a London club kid, enjoying the city's hot spots and off-the-hook nightlife.

"I got a place just behind the BT Tower," said Orlando, referring to London's famous Post Office Tower, "and I found my niche: clubbing and clothes!"

Orlando, who was quickly maturing into a six-foot-tall hottie, spent his nights at clubs with names like Kooky, Hollywood Babylon, and Billion Dollar Babes. Orlando has described the London clubs as "an amazing party scene with even more amazingly beautiful women, where everyone forgot about their job and became models or movie stars for the night."

So while Orlando was becoming a better actor by day, by night he also got to enjoy much of the big-city life that London had to offer.

Of course, to hang in these clubs, Orlando had to dress right. He became interested in fashion and created an original sense of style as a teen. "My best friend, Chris, his mum had a whole load of '60s clothes," Orlando said, "so we used to get dressed up in that stuff."

Orlando and his friends would also stake out the best boutiques in London, hunting down some new fashion line or a rare breed of sneaker just arrived from Japan. His sister, Samantha, also helped nurture his love of clothes by dragging him to top London fashion outlets such as Exfam. She would "throw suede jackets and flared trousers on me," Orlando reports. And he loved every minute of it!

But he had to find a way to pay for his lifestyle. Orlando held down various day jobs as well, including work at the ultra-hip fashion stores Box Fresh and Paul Smith. He could rarely afford the fashions he wanted. But that didn't stop him from longing for the stylistic touches that he would one day be able to purchase without thinking.

While much of his time was spent enjoying

London's cultural life, he also did a little bit of reading, including diving into a legendary series of fantasy books by J. R. R. Tolkien—*The Lord of the Rings* trilogy.

Ironically, though, he didn't make it all the way through the trilogy.

"I got halfway through the second book," said Orlando, "but then I got more interested in girls, cars, and sports."

Overall, the time in London was key for Orlando—a tremendous growth period in his life. It was a time when he was able to hang out with a lot of older people, learn about the world, and, as he puts it, "experience a lot of life at a young age."

When he turned 18, Orlando earned a scholarship to the British American Drama Academy (BADA), where many famous actors, including *Friends* star David Schwimmer, have studied and where great actors like Jeremy Irons and Kevin Spacey have taught.

With each passing year, Orlando's talent and popularity grew in leaps and bounds. Already working hard and getting cast in lots of great plays, Orlando was poised to jump to the next level.

Around this time, he starred in a play called *A Walk in the Vienna Woods*, and a film agent happened to be in the audience. The agent signed Orlando, and at the age of 20, Orlando was cast in his very first film role: a one-line part in the film *Wilde*, starring Jude Law and Stephen Fry.

While the part was minor, it attracted the attention of several casting directors, who saw potential in the talented and sexy young actor. But Orlando has always been a shrewd player who understands the importance of the quality of his work. Agents and casting directors soon began offering him lots of small roles, similar to the one in *Wilde*, but Orlando was determined to get as much acting education as possible. More than anything, he wanted to learn how to become the best actor he could be. So Orlando did something daring, something that up-and-coming actors rarely do. He turned down all the parts he was being offered.

Most actors in his position would have been thrilled to take whatever tiny TV or movie roles they could get, but Orlando understood that ultimately, these small parts wouldn't have made him a better, more famous, or more successful actor.

Instead Orlando attended a three-year program at the prestigious Guildhall School of Music and Drama, whose alumni also include Ewan McGregor, Joseph Fiennes, and Ben Chaplin.

Orlando studied his heart out during his time at Guildhall and earned his acting credits the same way all the great, legendary British actors have done—on the stage.

"I wasn't influenced by the offers," Orlando explained. "I always planned to go to drama school. I suppose I could have trained in the industry more. But instead, I chose an environment that would be more conducive to experimenting."

While at Guildhall, Orlando performed in many of the classics, including Chekhov's *The Seagull*, *Three Sisters*, and *Uncle Vanya*; Ibsen's *Peer Gynt*; Euripides' *The Trojan Women*; Sophocles' *Antigone*; and William Shakespeare's *Twelfth Night*.

Orlando's years at Guildhall were some of the most important years of his life and were, in many ways, the years he really grew up.

"I needed grounding. I needed an education in an industry that I wanted to be working in," said Orlando, who credits this time with not only teaching him the creative process, but also with giving him the opportunity to make the mistakes that every professional has to make early on.

"I learned to work with a company of actors and to work with a bit more, I hope, integrity than I would have done otherwise," he said. "That's probably what kept me round in the head, getting the chance to mess it up in the safety of an environment where it's all about education and growing and learning."

Part of what makes acting school a fun and bizarre experience is that some of the exercises the students do seem incredibly silly. In reality, they are important for developing the ability to portray the emotions and mannerisms of others, but in the moment, they can seem completely absurd.

One of the exercises Orlando did in school, for instance, required him and his classmates to mimic the movements and expressions of animals.

"We went to the zoo to study animals," recalls Orlando, "and the teacher asked, 'What animal do you want to be?' I think I wanted to be an ape, but she said, 'No, you're going to be a lizard because you need to learn to be still and find that stillness.'"

While the last animal most of us would compare Orlando to is the big, hairy ape, we can certainly see him as the slick, quick-tongued lizard, an animal that has always had a certain slyness about it (much like a certain on-screen elf Orlando would play in the years to come).

Throughout his tenure at Guildhall, Orlando

focused on his education. His refusal of screen work would end soon enough, and the part of a lifetime was on its way.

But before Orlando would land a role in one of the greatest movies of all time, his daredevil, adventure-loving tendencies would come close to not only ending his career, but his life as well!

CHAPTER THREE
A TERRIFYING FALL

Orlando always had a flair for danger. He is a sucker for any activity that gets his adrenaline pumping, anything that gives him a wild physical thrill.

So as one might expect, Orlando has been no stranger to broken bones over the years. His adventures have led to him to fracture his nose and legs, an arm, finger, and wrist, several ribs, and even his skull—*three times!*

But Orlando's scariest incident didn't come during a fun-filled, thrill-seeking adventure. The scariest moment of his entire life was the result of a simple accident.

Orlando was spending a relaxing Sunday having lunch at a friend's house. The door to his friend's roof terrace was warped and couldn't be opened from the inside. It needed a kick from the outside to make it work. Ever the eager beaver, Orlando volunteered for the job. But how could he get up to the roof to kick the door in?

Orlando crawled out his friend's window and climbed up about four or five feet to the roof. To support himself, he stood on a drainpipe. But as he soon found out, the pipe wasn't sturdy. It buckled under the full weight of his body, and he was sent crashing three terrifying stories, landing with a sudden *Whap!* between several iron railings and an old washing machine.

The fall not only knocked him unconscious—it broke his back.

A helicopter flew in to transport Orlando to the hospital, but once there, the copter had nowhere to land! So authorities on the scene needed to come up with a way to get Orlando out safely and quickly. In the end, they hooked Orlando up to a crane and lifted him out of the helicopter.

Once at the hospital, the doctors examined him—and gave their terrible diagnosis: with four broken vertebrae, three broken ribs, and a bruised spinal column, the doctors told Orlando he would probably never walk again. There was a very good chance that for the rest of his days, Orlando would be a paraplegic.

"It was awful," recalls Orlando. "For about four

days, I was contemplating that as a serious part of reality. Imagine having four nurses to move you, wash you, do everything for you. You lose your sense of dignity. My mum was so distraught."

Lying in his hospital bed, Orlando got a good, hard look at what the rest of his life might be like. Needless to say, he was petrified.

Four days after the accident, Orlando underwent surgery. The doctors cut his back open and bolted metal plates to his spine. Following the operation, the most optimistic prognosis the doctors could give him was that for the rest of his life, he would have severe nerve or bone damage.

But Orlando found he had an inner strength that was hard to squelch—even in the most trying and desperate of circumstances. In the face of fear and hopelessness, Orlando never lost faith that things would turn out all right and that he would walk again. His strong and supportive family was there for him every step of the way.

Any doctor who underestimated Orlando's inner fortitude was misguided. His recovery was quicker and more thorough than anyone could have imagined and might seem nearly miraculous.

Just 12 days after the horrifying accident, after doctors told him he might never walk again,

Orlando limped out of the hospital on crutches.

He had recovered, and his life would soon be back on track.

Even with his incredible rebound, the accident was a pivotal moment in Orlando's life. "That accident took me to a dark place," he said, struggling with the memory. "It was kind of the making of me, really. I feel like it really tested my belief in myself and everything else, because they told me I'd be in a wheelchair.

"I couldn't remember how to walk," Orlando said, recalling his therapy after the operation. "I literally couldn't remember whether to do toe, ball, heel or heel, ball, toe. It was bizarre."

Orlando figured it out soon enough, however, and his miraculous recovery continued to progress with astonishing speed. Orlando understood exactly how lucky he was and appreciated every glorious moment.

"Nothing is as terrific as . . . walking on your own for the first time," explained Orlando. "The doctors said I wouldn't be able to ever walk again, but I did. I believe to do so you need a lot of discipline and a fighter nature and the will not to give in. It was a terrible time, but on the other hand, I learned through that to value some things more. There are so many things we take for granted. Such an experience puts a lot into the right light. That, you can believe me."

Orlando reminds himself of the experience whenever his life hits a rough path.

"It was pretty dark and scary, but in many ways it was a blessing in disguise," said Orlando, "because at the time, I was a drama student living in London and kind of racing through life, impatient to be out and working. This really made me stop and pay attention and learn to enjoy life while it was happening. It's like I was so close to losing everything that everything I have now is a bonus."

Orlando also took a close look at the type of person he had been and realized that he didn't completely like what he saw. "This time let me become modest," he says. "The more obstacles you have to overcome, the more you grow as a human being."

Orlando will, of course, never forget that time, partly because he may never be completely free of the pain. As he will say in his British accent, his back still gives him "gyp." But he had the wits and strength to turn the experience into "a wake-up call to life and responsibility," and declares that the fact that he survived and continued to act has given him "a whole new lease on life."

"It was one of the most profound things to happen to me. To have time to contemplate your life and make something positive out of the experience—it changed the way I approach everything in life. My back," he has said, "is a constant reminder of how lucky I am."

That doesn't mean Orlando has given up thrill seeking entirely. He's just learned to be a little more . . . thoughtful about things. "I thought about buying a motorbike recently," Orlando said, "and I decided against it. I don't need to break any more bones. It's like, everything is going great. Why throw something like that in the mix and jeopardize it all?"

So now, with a new appreciation for his life's value, Orlando was about to gain one of the most amazing experiences any actor could ever hope for—the role of a lifetime!

CHAPTER FOUR
LEGOLAS:
THE PRINCE OF MIRKWOOD

In 1998, New Line Cinema announced one of the most adventurous projects in film history. Director Peter Jackson, previously known for a critically acclaimed but low-budget film called *Heavenly Creatures*, was going to film J. R. R. Tolkien's legendary *The Lord of the Rings* trilogy.

What made the project so outrageous was that Jackson was planning to film all three movies in one massive, 18-month-long shoot. New Line would then release the films over three consecutive Christmases, from 2001 to 2003.

The risk for New Line was incredible. The cost of the endeavor was estimated at anywhere from $270 to $360 million. If the first film were to flop, the entire company's success for 2002 and 2003 would be in question. Hundreds of millions of dollars would be wasted, and the future of New Line itself might even be placed in jeopardy.

Adding to the risk was the fact that director Jackson's previous experience was with much smaller films. His largest production before *Rings* was *The Frighteners*, a 1996 horror film starring Michael J. Fox. *The Frighteners* cost only $30 million to put together. So Jackson was venturing into brand-new territory, with no real proof that he could handle a production anywhere near this large.

And as if all of this wasn't enough, there was one final hurdle: *The Lord of the Rings* books had a built-in fan base that could just as easily work *against* the films as *for* them. If fans loved the first film, *The Fellowship of the Ring*, then the future of the next two films seemed rosy. But if fans disliked anything about the first film, the backlash could be harsh. The word *fan* originally derives from the word *fanatic*, and *The Lord of the Rings* devotees were just the type of people that word applied to. *Lord of the Rings* fans are intense, dedicated, and die-hard. So everything about the production had to be *perfect*.

Jackson decided to shoot the series in New Zealand. Not only did it have the kind of lush scenery that could pass for the Middle-Earth setting of *The Lord of the Rings*, but shooting in New

Zealand would be much cheaper than filming in Hollywood.

With the location settled, Jackson's greatest challenge would be finding the right cast.

The main actors needed to be strong enough to handle the grueling, physical 18-month shoot. They needed to be famous enough to attract attention, yet not so famous that their celebrity would distract viewers from the story. And they needed to be not just believable, but tailor-made for their roles.

Peter Jackson put out the word, and a massive, three-continent casting process was under way. He looked all over the world for actors, hiring casting directors from America, England, Australia, and New Zealand to fill the all-important roles.

Orlando, meanwhile, continued to perform in plays throughout London. He was now in his last year at Guildhall. While the back injury was behind him, he often took on roles that required a certain stillness so he wouldn't have to move around a lot. He later said that this experience would help him greatly in playing a patient and wise Elven warrior.

A casting agent who was familiar with Orlando got him a chance to audition for the role of Faramir of Gondor, brother of Boromir. For Orlando, the audition, while exciting, wasn't exactly a tremendous deal since just about everyone he knew from Guildhall was auditioning for one part or another, and having an audition was a long way from landing a role.

So Orlando taped an audition for Faramir as requested. Several months later, Jackson and his collaborator and wife, Fran Walsh, came to London. Orlando met them while they were in town and did a more formal audition, this time with Jackson directing him.

Shortly afterward, Orlando received the call he was waiting for from his agent. Unfortunately, he did not hear what he had hoped. The agent told him he would not be cast as Faramir. That part would go to an Australian actor named David Wenham, who had appeared in the films *Dark City* and *Moulin Rouge*.

Orlando only had one second to be disappointed because, as his agent soon told him, Jackson was not turning him down outright. Instead he requested that Orlando read for another role—the role of Legolas, the Elf prince of Mirkwood, an expert archer and one of the main members of the Fellowship of the Ring!

Orlando returned to the *Lord of the Rings* books that he failed to finish years earlier, and when he read up on Legolas, he was overjoyed. The role of Faramir was a smaller role that wouldn't even appear until the second film. Legolas, on the other hand, was a major part, a lead role throughout the trilogy!

So Orlando auditioned yet again, taking the next step in what would be, by the end, a six-month process.

While he was delighted with the opportunity to audition, Orlando wasn't optimistic about his chances for getting the part. After all, he was still a drama school student, just on the verge of graduation, with very little film experience. What chance did he have at this early stage of his career of being cast in such a major production?

Finally graduation approached. Orlando had completed his three years of training at Guildhall. Between that and his time at BADA and NYT, he felt ready to go out into the acting world—prepared, educated, and in full control of his craft. He would hit the streets, take in a full schedule of auditions for TV and movie parts, and work whatever odd jobs he needed to on the side to support the career he loved.

But two days before he was set to graduate, that all changed.

Orlando got the call. He was cast as Legolas.

"It was a moment in time that is forever crystallized for me," remembered Orlando. "My agent called and told me, 'I've got some news. You've been offered *The Lord of the Rings*.' I was over the moon."

Orlando's delight could hardly be contained. "I said 'absolutely!'" he explains. "I got the offer and I was freaking out and screaming and yelling. It was too much. I was 22 years old and I was about to complete acting school when they offered me the part. Suddenly I had a career coming my way."

This was, without question, the pivotal moment of Orlando's young career. The years of hard work and training had paid off much quicker than he had any right to expect. Twenty-two-year-old Orlando Bloom, not even officially out of drama school, was on his way to super-stardom.

"Anyone and everyone went on tape to try and have a part and be involved with that movie," explained Orlando. "For a young actor like me to have the opportunity to have 18 months in front of a camera working with Peter Jackson and that caliber of cast and crew was just unheard of. It was the opportunity of a lifetime."

Oddly enough, he received another call the very next day, asking if he wanted to tape a new episode of *Midsomer Murders*. Orlando couldn't help but laugh. As the saying goes, when it rains, it pours.

Orlando has compared being cast in *The Lord of the Rings* to winning the lottery, and that was true in more ways than one. Not only was getting the film an amazing break for him, but so was landing the role of Legolas instead of Faramir.

If Orlando had been cast as Faramir, would his career have emerged the same way? Would he have been seen prominently enough to make him the world-renowned heartthrob we all know and love? Would he have generated the acclaim that later led to roles in such films as *Pirates of the Caribbean* and *Troy*?

There's no way to know the answers to these questions. Perhaps his talent and good looks would have made him impossible to ignore, but Hollywood is a town where luck plays an undeniable role. We can all be thankful that Peter Jackson and his casting directors had an incredible eye for talent and knew that Orlando Bloom was too good not to place in a major role. As Legolas, Orlando was about to take both the movie world and a legion of adoring fans by storm.

CHAPTER FIVE
THE JOURNEY THROUGH
MIDDLE-EARTH

Taking on the role of Legolas meant pulling up roots for Orlando. While it would not be his first big move, it would mean a transition much larger than the previous one. After all, he wasn't just going from Canterbury to London. This time he was transporting himself halfway across the world, spending 18 months in New Zealand.

While Orlando was leaving a lot behind— including his mother, his sister, and his beloved dog, Maude—he had no idea what he was about to gain: a cast full of mates, co-conspirators, and true friends.

Orlando flew from London to New Zealand with his cast mate Elijah Wood. The two excited young actors passed the time by reading passages of *The Lord of the Rings* to each other.

Elijah had earned the lead role of Frodo Baggins. At five-foot six, with wide-set blue eyes, Elijah was cast not only for his immense talent, but for his youthful appearance, which was key to playing a child-like Hobbit.

Despite Elijah's young look and age (he was only 19 at the start of filming), he was already an experienced film actor. He started in show business when he was seven and by the time he was cast as Frodo had appeared in films like *Back to the Future II*, *Internal Affairs*, *The Ice Storm*, *The Faculty*, *Deep Impact*, and *Black and White*. The rest of the cast included show biz veterans with a similar history of solid performances.

Sean Astin, who had been seen in *The Goonies*, *War of the Roses*, *Bulworth*, and *Rudy*—and who had actually been nominated for an Oscar for a short film he himself produced and directed—was tapped for the role of Sam Gamgee, Frodo's trusted accomplice.

Sean Bean, from *Patriot Games* and *GoldenEye*, was Boromir of Gondor. Cate Blanchett, nominated for an Oscar for her starring role in *Elizabeth*, would portray the Elf queen Galadriel. Veteran actor John Rhys-Davies (*Raiders of the Lost Ark*) would play the dwarf Gimli. Finally, two of Britain's most highly acclaimed actors, Sir Ian Holm and Sir Ian McKellen, would play

Bilbo Baggins and Gandalf the Wizard in the films.

Fans of Tolkien's books applauded these choices, but not all the casting went so smoothly. Some fans were critical of the choice of Liv Tyler as the beautiful Elf Arwen, questioning her selection on bulletin boards all over the Internet. (That opinion would quickly change after the release of the first film.) And Stuart Townsend, who had been chosen as Aragorn, the ranger who eventually becomes king of Gondor, was replaced after the first week of filming.

Peter Jackson wasn't certain that Townsend could summon the strong presence necessary for the part. He was replaced with Viggo Mortensen, who would wow audiences with a dazzling and powerful performance.

The cast was now set, and Orlando would be working alongside some of the finest actors of his day. As he flew across the world to begin the job of his dreams, he must have realized that the education he just completed would be nothing compared to the one he was about to begin.

Once in New Zealand, Orlando immediately began training vigorously for his role. The Elf Legolas was an immortal—a 2,931-year-old warrior.

He was an expert rider and archer with super-human strength and the reflexes of a cheetah. Orlando knew he needed to be in the best shape possible to learn the skills that an elf would possess. And for someone as addicted to thrill sports as Orlando, the experience couldn't have been more exciting.

Orlando started with two months of training in archery, swordplay, and horseback riding. "The first thing they did was put a bow in my hand!" Orlando recalled. "I started using the bow and getting to grips with archery, so that by the end of the week I was taking paper plates out of the sky and trying to get some real dynamic movement into the way I used the bow."

Orlando saw the bow and arrow as an extension of Legolas's body, so he felt a responsibility to be truly proficient in that area. "By the time shooting was under way," he bragged, "I could fire an arrow whilst riding horseback."

Besides the bow work, Orlando knew that part of inhabiting a character completely is determining the character's physical movement. So he decided that a large part of his preparation should focus on establishing Legolas's specific fighting style.

As an immortal warrior with super-sharp senses,

Legolas was one who had seen it all and knew what it took to win in battle. He was fearless and unflappable, defined by strength and honor. He would remain calm and focused in the face of the most horrific evil, with the fortitude to overcome any adversity.

While attempting to summon inspiration for the character, Orlando realized that Legolas reminded him of the legendary samurai warriors of Japan—fighters who could face down any opponent with supreme confidence and wisdom.

Orlando decided to learn about the samurai and integrate their ways into Legolas's movement. He watched a Japanese movie called *The Seven Samurai,* which was directed by Akira Kurosawa, to learn how the ancient Japanese samurai walked and how they held their bodies. Orlando adopted the ways of the samurai to give Legolas the "aura of centeredness and focus" that is evident in his performance.

In addition to developing Legolas's movements, Orlando also needed to excel in swordplay and knife spinning. For this, he had one of the best trainers in the business.

Bob Anderson had worked in Hollywood for decades and had trained everyone in swordplay and knife fighting from Darth Vader to old-time *Robin Hood* actor Errol Flynn!

Orlando found his time with Bob fascinating.

"Bob has some stories to tell. He's a genius," confided Orlando. "My character has a couple of white knives on his back, which I had to learn to pull out and use."

In fact, not only did Orlando need to know how to fight with two blades at once, but in order to accommodate certain special effects, he needed to be able to fight and move with the knives *in slow motion* and still make it look impressive and showy for the camera!

With such expert training at his disposal, Orlando learned that all of these things were possible. In fact, his instruction was so good that he was able to replicate the rapid shooting of three arrows—one after the other—a feat that required lightning-quick movements (although the actual arrows were put in afterward as a special effect since real arrows tend to go off in all directions).

Orlando also received expert training in horseback riding since he rides for much of the films. He rode 20 different horses before finally being given the horse that he would ride during filming.

While he became something of an expert at horseback riding, Orlando still managed to do something during the shoot that he was already expert at . . .

He broke another bone.

It happened during the filming of a scene that featured 30 horses in a line. The horses had to ride over a mound and into a gully at top speed. The rocky surface had various dangers, including a steep downward slope. Jackson directed his cast to imagine that they were being attacked from behind by the Orcs, the monstrous villains of *The Lord of the Rings*. But things got a bit too exciting for the horses, and they reacted as one.

"I came off a horse," Orlando admitted. "We'd done this shot five times, and you have to imagine that the Orcs and Uruk-hai are around you and you are battering them down with your arrows. I had my hand on the rein and Brett Beattie (the stunt double for the character of Gimli) was behind me, and he had a horse that decided not to stop. I bailed and landed on a rock, and Brett landed on top of me."

Crunch! One of Orlando's ribs fractured.

But Orlando was barely fazed by the break. Doctors gave him medication for the pain, and he was working again within days.

In addition to the physical challenges, Orlando had another difficult task in New Zealand. In order to play Legolas, he had to learn a whole new *language*.

In creating the world of *The Lord of the Rings* as lovingly and painstakingly as he did, J. R. R. Tolkien invented an entirely new language for the Elves, which he called, appropriately, Elvish. The language is so difficult that three experts who were intimately familiar with it were kept on the set. They taught Elvish to the actors who needed it, including Orlando, and also taught parts of an Elvish dialect called Quenya (which was the language of the High Elves) to the cast members.

While he's always up for a challenge, learning Elvish was certainly not the easiest thing Orlando's ever done.

"It's a very difficult language to get your mouth around," said Orlando, who describes Elvish as having sort of a "Celtic/Welsh vibe."

"It's so hard to learn because there is nothing to hold on to with the Elvish language. The way that it flows, it sounds incredibly beautiful, but the emphasis is unnatural."

The actors relied on the language experts for

specific translations of phrases they needed to say.

"If we wanted to say something like, 'Watch your back,'" explained Orlando, "we'd have to write it down, and then they'd tell us how to say it."

Liv Tyler also had to learn Elvish, so she and Orlando became study partners and worked together to perfect it. Liv said that the language eventually became easy for her, rolling off her tongue as if she was possessed. But if Orlando didn't find it as easy as his co-star did, he did find it rewarding. By the end of the shoot, he was given a ring by his makeup artists, engraved with the phrase "to wherever it may lead" in Elvish.

As Orlando quickly learned on the set, Tolkien's in-depth creations meant that his portrayal of Legolas needed to be multidimensional and meaningful. He needed to really understand what Legolas was all about and, furthermore, what it meant to be a Tolkien elf.

Orlando immersed himself in the Tolkien books and soon became something of an expert on the subject. He learned that elves could never die in the sense that we think about death. That is, they couldn't be killed, nor were they affected by age. But they seemed to be in danger of passing from the earthly (or Middle-Earthly) plane. That's because Tolkien's elves were slowly passing from reality into mythology.

"Tolkien created them as the firstborn race," explained Orlando, "placed on Middle-Earth by the gods—so they have this otherworldly quality to them.

"The Elves were created by Tolkien to be the magical and mystical . . . capable of almost anything in terms of their abilities," said Orlando. "They have super-human strength, their reflex speed is incredible, their sensory awareness is amazing, and they are immortal. They're ageless."

And according to Orlando, as great as the Elves' capacity is for magic, so is their capacity for emotion. "They were created as angelic spirits," he said. "They have the greatest joy and the deepest sorrow."

Orlando used this information to create his version of who he thought Legolas would be. "I translated that into them always being centered, poised, and focused," said Orlando. He related that centeredness to the way so many people today "go to yoga classes and meditate and do all sorts of things to try to attain a higher state of mind and living."

This sense of stillness was so important to Legolas's character that Orlando even acted that way when they *weren't* shooting. "If the other Hobbit actors were joking around on set, I would usually be more quiet and still, trying to remain as focused and concentrated as I possibly could. I wanted that intensity in the character. It's all in the eyes, I think. It's not in what he says, it's in what he does—even if he's not running or fighting or shooting a bow. And if he does speak, it's because there's danger or something important that needs to be expressed. He'll say, 'The Orcs are about,' or, 'There's something unnerving about this situation. We need to move on.' That's his mission, his job."

"Legolas is a warrior," said Orlando. "He's an archer, and he becomes the eyes and ears of the Fellowship because elves don't sleep. If there's danger around, Legolas is the first to be aware of it—to let the Fellowship know. He's quite a cool little dude, really."

But if Orlando thought that Legolas was a cool little dude, he also came to realize just how important the character was to the legions of fans to whom *The Lord of the Rings* was an epic, a life-long favorite. There was a responsibility that came with portraying such a greatly loved character that Orlando never forgot.

"You wanted to do justice to the fan base," said

Orlando. "You didn't want to let these fans down, because I knew how much these books had meant to me as a kid—and I hadn't even finished reading all of them."

Orlando stopped at nothing to ensure the accuracy of the character. Since elves were forest-dwelling creatures, Orlando bought a book on trees and learned all he could about them. In fact, there was one point in which Orlando was so concerned with keeping Legolas authentic that it nearly got in the way of his performance.

"I was like, 'I've got to do everything I can because he's the character people have created in their imaginations over years.' But at one point, I said to myself—because I was so aware of it that it was actually blocking me—I said, 'I've gotta let go. I've been cast to play Legolas because I have some quality I can use to try to bring this character to life.' So I just do my best to do that."

Orlando wasn't the only one working his heart out to make Legolas as realistic as possible. *The Lord of the Rings* makeup and costume people were also toiling away, designing the look for the elves and the other characters and changing the actors' appearances on-screen to make them believable as the creatures of Middle-Earth.

While Orlando looked slightly different as Legolas, he didn't look any less gorgeous. Nothing was done to hide his perfect face or his well-defined cheekbones. He wore a long blond wig that cost $15,000 and was made of real hair. His olive complexion was made paler by makeup, and his deep brown eyes were covered with blue contact lenses, making them even more piercing than usual.

But he did have to alter his appearance in one major way. In order to get the wig to fit correctly, Orlando needed to shave his gorgeous head of hair!

In the end, though, he decided not to shave it completely. On set, Orlando was having his makeup done and the makeup people were raising his hairline for the full elf effect. At this point, Liv showed up for her own time in the artist's chair. She suggested that Orlando shave his hair at the sides, adding, "You'd look really cute in a Mohawk."

Taken by her suggestion and perhaps at the bit of flattery, Orlando got the Mohawk. He kept it for the entire length of the shoot.

One of the things Orlando fans are most curious about is the adorable Elf ears that were a part of the Legolas costume. They took two hours every day to put on, and once they were on, the makeup artists wanted them to *stay* on. While the ears weren't uncomfortable, they did present some problems.

"I went home one day without the wig, but with the ears on, because I had a four-hour break and it was the middle of the night," said Orlando. He fell asleep, and when he woke up, one of his ears was stuck to his pillow, while the other remained perfectly in place on his head!

Orlando also had to be very careful about where he wore his ears since the cast needed to make sure they weren't photographed in costume. "I'd love to have gone out with them on," he said, "but we had tight security." To go out on break without taking off the ears, Orlando would have had to wear a hooded jacket or sweatshirt everywhere he went.

But as with most of the things happening on the set, Orlando had fun with it because he wasn't alone in the experience. All the cast members had to undergo some sort of makeup/costuming ordeal on a daily basis. All the Elves, for example, had to deal with the problem of glue in their ears.

Liv Tyler has said that while they would take

the ears on and off on a daily basis, they never really got *all* the glue off, so the Elves would walk around constantly picking glue out of their ears.

"I went home to New York," said Liv, "and a week later I still had all this sticky stuff. I was at a party, picking my ears and going, 'Ooh, sorry.'"

While the elves had sticky ears to worry about, the actors playing the Hobbits had the infamous Hobbit feet glued on every day. Liv said that hanging out with the cast during a night on the town would be amusing, because "the Hobbits would be picking their feet and the Elves would be picking their ears."

The challenge of managing glue, though, was relatively minor. More important and difficult was keeping track of which part of the script was being shot each day. Movies are usually filmed out of sequence since it's easier to shoot all the scenes at one location before moving on. This can be challenging for actors. Imagine having a script and shooting the beginning and then the end while skipping the middle. It can be confusing.

Now imagine if there were not one, but *three* very long, complicated scripts to contend with. You might actually film parts of the first script in the morning and parts of the last one at night!

This would become one of the most frustrating aspects of the shoot for Orlando. "That was the thing that was most challenging," he confessed. "We might be doing the third movie in the afternoon and the first movie in the morning. Keeping on top of everything was like juggling."

Orlando said it became a "nightmare" at times trying to keep track of where they were in the story. To make it seem like the character knew where he was and why, Orlando (and all the other actors) kept Tolkien's books nearby. The books became their bible, and they referred to them frequently.

"It was like homework going home every night, keeping track of where you were in the story," he said. But all of these "hardships" just added to the experience for Orlando and his cast mates.

Living in New Zealand for that year and a half was a life-changing experience for all involved, and Orlando absolutely fell in love with both his co-stars and New Zealand.

"It wasn't easy to be away from my family," said Orlando, "but I found a new family in New Zealand. I loved it! After all those months, it felt like home. It's so beautiful. The people are incredibly nice, and anywhere you go, it's just mind-blowing, dramatic scenery. So I feel very fortunate to have had that time with these people and to have made some very good friends."

Not surprisingly, Orlando wasted little time taking advantage of New Zealand's wondrous outdoor terrain. Within days of the cast settling in New Zealand, it was clear that Orlando was going to be the daredevil of the group. And while the film's producers warned the cast to avoid any dangerous activities that could cause production-disrupting injuries, Orlando couldn't be stopped. New Zealand offered him the chance to indulge the adrenaline junkie inside him.

"There was a memo that was sent round during filming saying, 'We're going down to Queenstown, it's the adventure capital of New Zealand, so please don't do anything stupid. Don't bungee jump, skydive, white-water raft, etc.' I sort of ignored it," Orlando admits. "Within two hours I had thrown myself off the first bungee jump in the town, and I was on my own, which is scary because you haven't got your mates goading you on to make you do it."

But having to go it alone didn't stop Orlando. In addition to an incredibly enriching acting experience, his time in New Zealand allowed him to develop a real passion for thrill sports. "New Zealand is the place where they invented the bungee." Orlando grins. "I love that!"

Many people consider Orlando's love of extreme sports fearlessness, but he says that's not completely the case. He describes his instinct for danger as more a matter of *confronting* fear than conquering it.

"Don't get me wrong, I'm terrified of standing on a ledge and jumping off," said Orlando. "But you confront that fear and get over it and it empowers you in some way. When you're standing in front of a 150-foot drop with a piece of cord tied to your ankles, it's scary. I knew it was something that I would be afraid of, but I really wanted to try it. I went mad for it."

Orlando got to try several exciting things for the first time in New Zealand, including skydiving, white-water rafting, and a bizarre and scary stunt called "fly-by-wire," which allows the user to fly so quickly that he or she actually experiences weightlessness. "I like anything dangerous," he says. "One day, I did the highest bungee jump in New Zealand five times in the space of half an hour!"

Of course, since the film's producers wouldn't be too thrilled about Orlando taking these risks, he was careful not to tell them until after the fact.

Meanwhile the cast was quickly becoming a tight-knit unit, and they discovered early on that they genuinely cared about each other. Soon Orlando wanted to share his love of adventure with his new friends.

"When I arrived in Wellington," said Orlando, "I wanted to find some sort of extracurricular activity we could do outside *Lord of the Rings*, just to keep us sane." Orlando suggested mountain biking and fly-by-wire, but his cast mates seemed eager to stay free from injury.

"I was like, 'Let's get motorbikes!' and the guys weren't into that at all," said Orlando. "They were like, 'There's no need to kill ourselves while we're working on this.'"

But when Orlando suggested surfing, he finally found something that everyone could enjoy.

"Billy Boyd [who played Pippin] was into it, so that day we bought boards and went down to Lyall Bay," said Orlando. "We walked onto the beach with these brand-new, sparkling boards, freshly waxed, and in our new little wet suits. The other surfers were looking at us like we were idiots! And the water was freezing."

Orlando and Billy hit the waves and promptly fell off the boards, but it didn't matter because they had a great time—at least, when Billy wasn't freaking out.

Once while surfing at night, Billy saw a seal's flipper and mistakenly thought it was the fin of a great white shark. While Billy began to unravel, Orlando hid his fear as best he could and immediately put himself between Billy and harm's way.

Soon enough, several of the *Lord of the Rings* cast—including Elijah, Sean, Billy, and Dominic Monaghan (who played Merry)—were surfing on a regular basis. Over time, Orlando and the boys branched out, enjoying snowboarding, white-water rafting, and yes, even bungee jumping.

"We sampled everything the country has to offer," said Orlando. "The weirdest things to throw yourself off are in New Zealand."

Of course, someone *did* eventually get hurt. On the day they persuaded Viggo Mortensen, the 43-year-old actor who played Aragorn, to join them surfing, he wound up with a black eye. So all of the scenes he filmed the following day—the scenes in the mines of Moria for *The Fellowship of the Ring*—had to be done with Viggo shot from the side.

They say a person can only court danger so long before finding it. And a place like New

Zealand has so many ways to find adventure that there surely must be some dangerous aspects to it. So while *The Lord of the Rings* shoot was tons of fun, it also had many pitfalls.

For one thing, the cast had to deal with sand flies, which Orlando described as "the nastiest of insects."

"Their bite is bad," he explains, "and it lasts for ages." Of course, the *Lord of the Rings* producers made sure there was lots of insect repellent on hand. But not even the most influential Hollywood producers had the power to repel *landslides*.

In one harrowing incident, Orlando took a car ride with actor Sean Bean, who played Boromir. The two were heading toward New Zealand's South Island for filming. Since Sean disliked flying, Orlando had agreed to drive with him instead. In the midst of the ride, rain started falling—not in drops, but in buckets. "You've never seen so much rain," said Orlando. "I was videoing it and thinking, 'This is insane.'"

After nine hours of continuous torrential downpour, the roads became all but invisible. Then at one frightening moment, Orlando and Sean saw a landslide coming right for them! Orlando tells the story:

"We spun the car around, but we ran straight into another landslide farther up the road. So we pulled into this petrol station where there was already a queue of people. We managed to find a little cottage where they let us stay. They had to carry us out in a helicopter, in all this torrential rain, which was kind of hairy. Sean was gutted [incredibly upset]. He'd done this whole drive just to avoid the flight."

But while Orlando's time in New Zealand had its share of hard moments, overall it was incredibly rich and rewarding. Not only was New Zealand a great country for adventure, but it was a gorgeous and inspiring place to spend a year and a half.

The house that Orlando stayed in—just around the corner from Peter Jackson's house—was on a beautiful bay on a series of cliffs, with the sea directly in his view. Liv Tyler stayed in a similar house nearby. "You wake up to rainbows and dolphins," Liv recalls. "So, we had each other and work and some of the most beautiful scenery I've ever seen."

Orlando loved the country so much that he, Elijah, Dominic, and Billy actually considered buying a house there to use as a permanent vacation spot. Orlando the romantic saw New Zealand as a place to possibly have a family and a great spot to one day raise his children.

In addition to the wondrous location, part of what made the shoot so unique was that New Zealand had never hosted a production of such incredible size and scope. The crew included over 2,500 people! And the producers used many New Zealanders as crew or extras. Locals were employed for everything from blowing glass to making baskets, building boats to making boots, sewing clothes to repairing roofs. Every profession imaginable was put to work to create the sets, costumes, weapons, armor—even the villages themselves.

The amount of support given the production from the citizens of New Zealand was unheard of. It was as if everyone in the country made the actors and crew a part of their family.

But New Zealand's dedication went further than just providing a dedicated workforce. When Jackson needed an army of extras for a battle scene, for example, the government sent in an army—the *real* army!

The production was so important to New Zealand that the country actually appointed a government official whose title was "Minister of *The*

Lord of the Rings." His job was to use the attention New Zealand got from the filming to attract other business to the country.

While his job was entirely serious, having a job with the title "Minister of *The Lord of the Rings*" would certainly bring a smile to anyone's face!

After the production ended, the country issued a special set of *Lord of the Rings* stamps featuring several of the cast members, including Orlando. Sir Ian McKellen joked that "everyone sending their Christmas card is going to lick our backsides and put us on the envelope." But of course, he recognized that the wonderful and possibly ground-breaking relationship between his production and this country was no joke. "That's how much it means to New Zealand," said Sir Ian. "*Lord of the Rings* is really part of their life and culture now."

As great as the mutual admiration was between New Zealand and *The Lord of the Rings*, the individual cast members loved each other just as much. The friends Orlando made on the set of *Lord of the Rings* will be his friends for life.

Orlando and Viggo, for example, became extremely close. As filming progressed, the two took to mocking each other about their status in the film. Since Orlando played an elf and Viggo played a human, Viggo (or "Vig," as Orlando called him) would call Orlando "Elf boy," and Orlando would call Vig "filthy human."

"As an Elf, I never got a scratch on me, never got dirty," said Orlando. "And Vig would come out with blood and sweat all over him. And he'd say to me, 'Oh, go manicure your nails.'"

The ribbing between the cast members was always good-natured, always in fun. "Viggo will go on about Elves and how they're always doing their nails and brushing their long, blond hair and being all prissy," said Orlando. "And I just say, 'Well, at least I'm going to live forever! Got that? LIVE FOREVER!'"

And, as would be expected from a group of mostly young men stuck far away from home for long periods, good-natured ribbing soon escalated to pranks. In fact, the older actors playing the humans (Vig and Sean Bean) declared a war of sorts on the Hobbits and Elves.

Several of the actors found the things inside their trailers tossed about. And at one point, Orlando was the victim of a relentless "assault" from both humans and Hobbits alike.

Viggo and Sean broke into Orlando's room in the middle of the night and carried him downstairs.

Billy and Dominic sat on his knees, and Sean pulled his arms back. Then Viggo pulled up his shirt and gave him belly slaps until his stomach was red.

And another time, Viggo had his son cover Orlando's trailer in duct tape.

But Orlando wasn't one to take all this lying down. Soon after the stomach slapping incident, a pile of rotten fish and fake poo mysteriously found its way into Viggo's trailer.

The endless joking was a product of the great bonds the cast had formed. To Orlando, it was as if the guys had become the brothers he never had. The cast members became *so* close, in fact, that they went to extraordinary lengths to ensure that they'd never forget the remarkable experience they shared.

The entire Fellowship of the Ring, save one, got the same tattoo.

Eight of the nine members of the fellowship—including 65-year-old Sir Ian McKellen—got tattooed with the Elvish symbol for the number nine. Not surprisingly, the tattoo was partly Orlando's idea.

Orlando proposed it to the others along with Dominic. Both thought that since tattoos were an important part of the Maori culture of New

Zealand, it would be an appropriate way to cement their friendship. While several of the cast members were hesitant, they ultimately understood the significance of the gesture and gave in— all except for John Rhys-Davies, the actor who played Gimli the Dwarf. (True to the film's spirit of camaraderie, however, John's stunt double stood in for him here as well and got the tattoo instead!)

As an indication of how the cast learned to enjoy every experience, the group made tattoo day into something of a party. Their only day off was Sunday, so they located someone who had a tattoo parlor and persuaded him to open up his shop. The cast took pictures of each other getting the tattoos, and Sean Astin even brought his wife and daughter, who were visiting at the time. Sean's daughter sat under the table and told him, "Daddy, if it hurts too much, you can come down here with me."

While they originally hoped to keep the tattoos a secret, word leaked out, and it soon became a favorite story for the press. "There are a lot of naughty Hobbits running around," said Sir Ian. "When we first had this done, it was agreed we would tell no one except those who are in a position to discover it for themselves. And now everyone is talking about it."

The cast members got the tattoos on different areas of their bodies. Orlando's is on his right forearm, a spot he picked because Legolas is the archer. (Only Elijah's is in a place you may not easily see on the beach—his is on the lower part of his abdomen.)

At one point, several of the cast members got a chance to compare their close bond with that of another, similar production. As it happened, *Star Wars, Episode II: Attack of the Clones* was shooting close by in Australia. About five months into filming, Orlando, Dominic, Billy, and Elijah took a week's vacation and visited the *Star Wars* set, hoping to hang with stars Hayden Christensen and Natalie Portman, among others.

While they all had fun, Elijah later said there was a slight sense of competitiveness between the two camps. "We felt like a rogue crew," he said. "There was a weird sense that with the two trilogies, there was this odd undercurrent of rivalry."

Apparently the *Star Wars* folks found it odd that the *Lord of the Rings* cast called each other "Hobbits" off the set. But that just re-emphasized how close the *Lord of the Rings* cast members had become.

"Within the first month, we *were* those characters," Elijah explained. "We called ourselves the Hobbits because we adopted the relationships that were important to those characters. We were always together. We were on set together, we went out for meals together, we loved being around each other."

While Orlando was an elf, he was definitely a part of the Hobbits crew—partly because the Hobbits were the youngest cast members and also partly because they all truly enjoyed each other's company. Spending the week with the *Star Wars* crew really drove home how close they had all become. When confronted with people from another production, even a production going through similar experiences, the others felt distant. Few could be as close to them as they were, at this point, to each other.

But while future productions might not find Orlando bonding with cast mates as closely, that's not to say that there wasn't even more excitement on its way.

When Orlando meets fans in the street, he is open and available, giving people as much time and attention as he can. He signs autographs, he chats, and he has even rubbed a pregnant fan's belly for luck. But when he's dating someone, he's a gentleman through and through. And that means no gossip and no parading his dates in front of the press or at public events. When it comes to dating and girlfriends, Orlando keeps his private life private.

While he was shooting *The Lord of the Rings,* Orlando had a girlfriend back in England. She would fly out to New Zealand to visit, and actually spent seven straight months there with Orlando at one point. Throughout that time Orlando never spoke about her to the press and never revealed her name to anyone outside his loyal circle of friends. But though he tried his best to protect the relationship, dating someone who is working halfway across the world can be hard on anyone. So toward the end of the shoot, Orlando and his girlfriend broke up.

By that point, Orlando was a bundle of mixed emotions. He was in the midst of one of the richest, most fulfilling experiences an actor could ever go through. He spent a year and a half with cherished friends he'd have his entire life. At the same time, though, he was saddened by the loss of his relationship and was learning how incredibly hard it can be to be a successful actor, filming in exotic locations around the world while trying to keep a loving relationship together.

"She was a really big love," Orlando said of the lucky mystery girl. "It's sad. I don't know what happened. We found it very difficult, so we split up." But while he was disheartened by the breakup, Orlando, who always tries to look on the bright side of things, managed to make that time a profound learning experience.

"I think it's something you have to learn to manage," he said. "The sad thing is, sometimes relationships will suffer. It isn't easy to be uprooted from your friends and family constantly, but I love what I'm doing."

Orlando admits that the relationship might

have worked had it not been his first time in this situation. "A big reason it didn't work out with my girlfriend was that it was new territory, and we didn't know how to deal with it. In hindsight, there were certain things I should've done, but you learn as you go."

In the end, Orlando showed his maturity, taking a very philosophical approach to the situation. "That's life," said Orlando. "People come into your life and people leave it. Certain things happen for a reason. You just have to trust that life has a road mapped out for you."

So for the time being, Orlando would be satisfied with being "married to his career" and would let relationships sort themselves out over time. Because his career would keep him so busy, this was probably a good thing.

The *Lord of the Rings* shoot ended in early 2001. Even though the first film, which would be called *The Lord of the Rings: The Fellowship of the Ring*, was almost a year away from being released, the production attracted enough attention that those involved were in demand in Hollywood. Orlando took a brief vacation—surfing in Florida with Hobbits Billy Boyd and Dominic Monaghan—and then went out to Los Angeles shortly afterward to meet with producers and directors about new projects.

It seemed Orlando's extraordinary luck was about to strike again because the very first meeting he had in L.A. was for a film called *Black Hawk Down*, directed by famed director Sir Ridley Scott (*Alien, Blade Runner, Gladiator, Thelma and Louise*). As it turned out, one meeting was all Orlando needed. Even though the producers were searching for actors all throughout America and Europe, Orlando got his part almost immediately. Just like that, he was cast in his next major film!

Black Hawk Down's producer, Jerry Bruckheimer, saw great things for Orlando.

"When the camera is on Orlando, he is so natural," says Jerry. "He's got that look, as if he could have come from another time."

But as hot as he was on the Hollywood radar screen, Orlando never got cocky. He was always humble and felt that despite his obvious talent and good looks, he was also enjoying a bit of good fortune.

"I've had some great opportunities," said Orlando. "For *Lord of the Rings*, I just happened to be around when they were looking for people who were slightly unknown that they could take and use for three movies. And with *Black Hawk Down*, I had just come into L.A. for the first time, and I got the part! I'm aware that there are hundreds of brilliant actors out there who need that opportunity. The fact that I got it is what I'm constantly thanking my lucky stars for."

Black Hawk Down told the true story of an American military mission that happened in the African country of Somalia in 1993. It was in the city of Mogadishu, where over 300,000 Somalis were starving to death. The mission was supposed to be simple and quick, taking about an hour. Instead it was a disaster. A vicious 15-hour battle occurred, and 18 American soldiers were killed. It was the worst ground battle for American troops since the Vietnam War.

Immediately after the skirmish, the bodies of some of the deceased U.S. soldiers were paraded through the streets of Somalia, and people worldwide saw this awful moment on television. The tragedy sickened Americans and wound up having a strong influence on American foreign policy.

Orlando was cast as Todd Blackburn, a U.S. Army private who falls from a helicopter and—can you believe this?—breaks his back. That's

As a student at London's Guildhall School of Music and Drama, Orlando had no idea how quickly his fame would skyrocket.

*O*rlando

Black Hawk Down was the world's introduction to Orlando Bloom. Right from the start Orlando proved to be both sexy and serious.

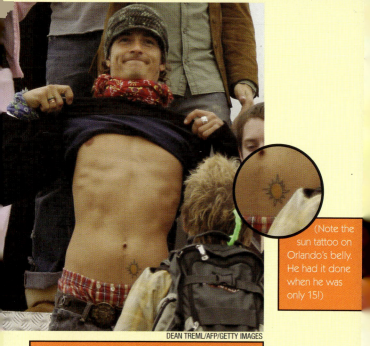

(Note the sun tattoo on Orlando's belly. He had it done when he was only 15!)

Orlando greets the crowd enthusiastically as the *Lord of the Rings* cast arrives in New Zealand.

Orlando developed an intense bond with his fellow cast members during the trilogy's year-and-a-half–long shoot, particularly with Viggo Mortensen, who played Aragorn. Viggo and Orlando gave each other nicknames like "Elf-boy" and "filthy human" and pranked each other endlessly on set.

*O*rlando

© NEW LINE CINEMA COURTESY THE EVERETTE COLLECTION

Orlando melts hearts and kicks butt as the arrow-slinging Elf Legolas.

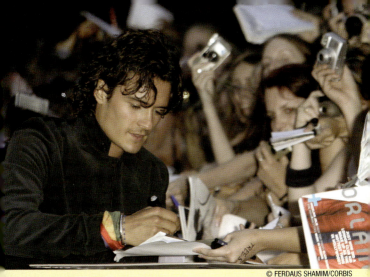

Orlando's performance in *The Lord of the Rings* earned him the adoration of thousands of fans.

At New Zealand's massive *Lord of the Rings* premiere party, Orlando and his co-star, the lovely Liv Tyler, wave to the crowd during the cast's ticker tape parade.

Orlando

Orlando on the set during the filming of *Pirates of the Caribbean*.

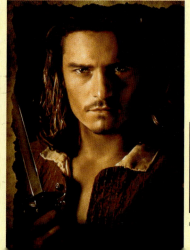

The moment *Pirates of the Caribbean* hit theaters, Orlando attained heartthrob status.

right, just a few short years after breaking his own back, Orlando played a character that does the same thing! The strange coincidence may well have been a deciding factor in his getting the part.

Only Orlando can turn broken bones into a career move.

"I had mentioned that had happened to me when I was up for the part," says Orlando. "Who knows why one actor gets a job and another doesn't? I think it was just good timing that I happened to be there and I had had the experience. I was lucky."

Orlando was cast alongside a host of talented actors, including Josh Hartnett and Ewan McGregor. His first scene was shot with Ewan, a fellow graduate of Guildhall. So in between takes, the two traded Guildhall stories, gossiping about teachers they had back at school.

Black Hawk Down was filmed in Morocco because actually filming in war-torn Somalia was impossible. Since Orlando was playing an American soldier, he needed to eliminate his British accent and speak like an American. There were several other British actors also playing Americans, so the director hired a dialect coach to work with them and make sure their natural British inflections didn't slip into their speech.

For Orlando, this was yet another great acting challenge to enjoy in his quest to be the best actor he could be. He worked hard, both with the coach and on his own, to make sure his American accent was accurate.

"I decided to speak in my American voice all day long so that I felt the voice was my own," said Orlando.

The speech work not only taught Orlando a lot about acting, but about Americans as well.

"Americans are very strong and focused in the way they communicate," Orlando explained, "whereas the Brits kind of offer something and then stop a bit. There's also a difference in the body language between the two nationalities. I had to learn to just kind of relax, whereas we're somewhat more formal in Great Britain."

With the part of Private Blackburn, a pattern in Orlando's roles was beginning to emerge. Legolas had been the strong, silent type; a brave man not afraid to sacrifice in battle to conquer evil. Private Blackburn was one of the U.S. Army's soldiers, sent into harm's way to do good. Clearly producers were starting to sense something about Orlando that lent itself to a certain strength and heroism. The stillness Orlando often spoke of when talking about Legolas was becoming a part of him. Although he's not a bulky guy, not overbearingly strong in the physical sense, there is still something about him that radiates inner strength.

In fact, while filming *Black Hawk Down*, Orlando learned that this stillness was prized in the U.S. Army—so prized that it was actually taught!

One of the Army Ranger slogans is "Slow is smooth, and smooth is fast," meaning that if you're just moving quickly and not paying attention to what's around you, you can't really see what you need to see. Orlando's style was smooth and fast, and producers were taking notice.

Orlando wasn't blind to that growing quality inside him and his relationship to these traits in others. As he learned about the American soldiers, he became very impressed by their sense of loyalty and sacrifice.

"The Rangers' code of conduct is that you never leave a man fallen or down," said Orlando. When his character, Private Blackburn, fell from the helicopter, the other soldiers' attempt to rescue him is what put them in position for the disaster ahead. Yet none would have ever questioned that attempt.

In a way, despite the obvious differences between *Black Hawk Down*'s harsh reality and the fantastic qualities of Middle-Earth, the sense of loyalty that coursed through both projects made them more thematically similar than one might expect.

The military trainers Orlando worked with on *Black Hawk Down* taught him that success in the military was about teamwork, about looking out for your fellow soldier to the point of risking your life, if necessary, for his survival—just as the Fellowship of the Ring had been a loyal, all-for-one and one-for-all group who would willingly die to protect each other.

One of Orlando's cast mates, Tom Sizemore, compared the Ranger experience to having "two hundred best friends, and every single one of them would die for you."

"They went into Mogadishu, did what they were trained to do, and put their lives on the line," said Orlando. "Anyone who puts themselves in that position succeeds on every level in my book."

So in addition to growing into a gorgeous man, Orlando was developing a strong sense of nobility.

But growing up didn't mean growing out of some of his favorite pleasures. Once again, Orlando got to enjoy some adventurous thrills—this time on the *Black Hawk Down* set.

The producers felt that for the battle scenes to look authentic, the actors needed to experience what it was like to be part of the military, even if only for a short time. So after the producers met with people from the U.S. Department of Defense (including the secretary of defense, one of the most powerful men in the country), the actors in *Black Hawk Down* took part in actual military training on real U.S. military bases. Their instructors were not only real military trainers, but some were the actual soldiers who participated in the Battle of Mogadishu and had been friends with the men who died there.

The training program was led by Harry Humphries, a former Navy SEAL who was highly decorated in Vietnam and had worked with the producer Jerry Bruckheimer on films like *The Rock, Con Air, Armageddon, Enemy of the State,* and *Pearl Harbor.*

Orlando and 20 of his fellow actors—all the actors who played the Rangers—went to Fort Benning in Georgia, where they underwent a modified version of the U.S. Army Ranger indoctrination program, or RIPIT, as it is called.

Orlando and his cast mates trained with the best instructors from the 75th Ranger Regiment. They learned about the loyalty and code of honor needed to be a good Ranger and also trained in actual combat and real-life survival skills. Plus they learned much about what really happened over those 15 horrific hours in Mogadishu from those who were there.

At the rate he was going, Orlando was on his way to becoming something of a combat expert. He already knew how to fight with swords, knives, and bows and arrows. Now he would get a first-hand glimpse at how modern soldiers fared in combat.

At Fort Benning, Orlando and his cast mates learned general military knowledge, like how to properly wear their uniforms and various military customs, including the Ranger Creed and Ranger history. They learned advanced marksmanship skills, including how to fire M16-A2 rifles and automatic weapons. They would go on five-mile runs, jump around on monkey bars, endure 20-foot falls, and even learn how to blow things up. They also learned used to use radios, tie knots, and engage in hand-to-hand combat.

At the end of the program, the "Rangers" had to make their way down the street of a mock village and avoid getting shot.

The thrills didn't stop once the training ended and the actual filming began. Orlando didn't need to find any bungee jumps on this shoot since every day was an extreme-sports adventure.

Orlando and three of his co-stars got to ride in a Little Bird, which is an American army helicopter flown by actual Army pilots. The copter flew them right over cliffs and down toward the sea.

"Those machines are so powerful!" exclaimed Orlando. The helicopter had no door, so the actors had their feet dangling out the side. At one point, the helicopter imitated zero gravity and fell straight down! "You freefall, and for a few seconds you're floating. You're weightless." Orlando said it was "the most freaky thing ever—close to walking on the moon, probably."

The helicopter ride was so exhilarating that according to Orlando's co-star Jason Isaacs, they all "screamed like four-year-olds." When they landed, they just jumped around, hugging each other and yelling, delirious with excitement about what they had experienced.

The entire enterprise was intense. While production on *The Lord of the Rings* had been big and spread out, the *Black Hawk Down* filming was akin to being in a fishbowl—surrounded on all sides by hot, dry, dusty, nonstop chaos.

Most of the film consisted of battle sequences, so director Ridley Scott wanted it to look as crazed and out of control as possible. When soldiers are in battle, that's how it really is.

"On *Black Hawk Down*, there was no messing around," said Orlando. "You had six to eight helicopters in the air, six to eight cameras filming, 600 to 800 people on set. It was a big machine, and there was a different type of approach to getting it on film. I was being baptized by fire and just trying to hold my own and keep it going."

For Orlando, who wore a typical Army-issue buzz cut to replace his blond *Lord of the Rings* mane, the chaos only made the experience that much more exciting.

"You didn't even have to act like you were getting shot because you were often getting paintballs fired all around you," said Orlando. "But it was fantastic. [As a kid] I used to run around with toy machine guns, wearing all that combat gear, and suddenly I'm being paid for it."

Orlando was exhausted and ready to head home by the end of the shoot but said that despite this, *Black Hawk Down* was fantastically rewarding. "As an actor, it was a great experience. I didn't have much to do, but I had my moments, and I learned a hell of a lot from working on such a huge machine of a set, which is how Ridley runs things."

And now, after four films' worth of intense, gratifying, life-changing experiences, Orlando was ready for a break.

CHAPTER SEVEN
TAKING A BREAK, THEN
BUSTING OUT

Orlando was now heavily in demand in Hollywood. A lot of scripts were sent his way. But as he read many of them, he found they shared one particular trait. They were, as the English might say, bloody awful.

The majority of screenplays were for "teen" movies—light, commercial films that would capitalize on Orlando's looks but wouldn't even come close to making use of his extensive, classical acting training.

Lord of the Rings and *Black Hawk Down* gave Orlando a growing reputation as a serious, talented actor. But there was also no getting around the fact that he was a heartthrob.

Once *Lord of the Rings* came out, legions of fans across the world would see him for his looks as well as his talent. As such, Orlando had two paths to choose from: take the easy roles offered to actors sought after for their looks or continue to challenge his ability with more serious parts.

After working so hard for so long to be a great actor, there was never even a question of which way Orlando would go. Toiling away in New Zealand and Morocco had made him a strong person who got stronger every year. And this was exactly what he wanted—to be a great actor, to work with other great actors (and great directors), and to constantly take on roles that would challenge him further, stretching his talent to its limits, if those even existed.

The pinup route was for someone else. Orlando was determined to go his own way.

It's not surprising, therefore, that when asked which actor's career he most wanted his to resemble, Orlando answered, "Johnny Depp. He's made some interesting choices and preserved his integrity. I admire that in an actor." Orlando also cites Edward Norton and Daniel Day-Lewis as favorites.

Orlando wanted to do work that had a message, work that, as he said, "casts a light over an area that's dark."

So he bided his time and read scripts, even contemplating possible stage work. After acting in four large-scale films, Orlando liked the idea of "doing something smaller."

To that end, Orlando did film two smaller roles in 2001 following *Black Hawk Down*. Unfortunately, neither of these movies, *Deed Poll* and *Lullaby of Clubland*, ever saw the inside of a theater.

Orlando did both of these movies for reasons that were clearly more personal than professional. *Deed Poll* was never even slated to be a studio release. It was a 40-minute, black-and-white experimental film he co-starred in with good friends of his—a German actor named André Schneider and an actress named Joanne Morley who had once dated Orlando.

In *Deed Poll*, Orlando and Joanne played an evil brother and sister who kill their parents. The difficult shoot for this simple 40-minute film took 34 days. The director didn't like Orlando's acting and actually wanted to fire him, but Orlando's friend André wouldn't film without him. Things came to a head when the director hit André in the face. In the end, the director was fired, Orlando stayed on, and a new director finished the film.

Orlando chose *Deed Poll* because it was a real acting challenge for him. His character was in many ways the complete opposite of the heroes he had been playing up to that point.

Lullaby of Clubland was similar. In that film too he played a darker character who gets involved in a sordid underworld. Orlando's friends André and Joanne co-starred in *Clubland* as well. Orlando's part was only on-screen for about seven minutes, but in the end it didn't matter—the production was plagued by disaster. Toward the end of filming, the director drowned. Four others involved with the film died over the next few months. The film was never released.

Orlando's choice to do those films proved once again that he wasn't afraid to take risks. Many people with blockbuster experience wouldn't take a chance on experimental films or roles that were darker and more personal. These two movies showed that Orlando was willing to stretch his talent and surprise his audience in order to do films that he found personally satisfying.

In the meantime, the question of his next big Hollywood enterprise wasn't one Orlando was in any hurry to answer—because the publicity machine for *Lord of the Rings* was revving up full steam!

Orlando and his cast mates started on a full schedule of interviews and photo shoots so that items about the movie could appear in the press that fall and through the film's December 2001 release. Orlando knew that despite his experience, the general public still hadn't seen much of him. He'd have to brace for the tidal wave of attention about to come his way.

Orlando and the cast traveled all around the world, talking to the media. Orlando began seriously appearing in the press around October. While many of the interviews were standard, he got some interesting assignments as well.

Orlando did a photo shoot for *Los Angeles Times Magazine* with Sean Astin and Sean Bean where he got to wear some of the season's top fashions. The public learned that while Orlando's idea of a wardrobe essential was an old pair of button-fly 702 Levi's, his favorite designers included Marc Jacobs, Gucci, and his former employer, Paul Smith. He told the *Times* that when it came to fashion, "I like to break the forms a bit by mixing them up with vintage pieces."

One of the delights of Orlando's approaching success would be his ability to indulge his growing passion for fashion. He had already had an interest in clothing pre–*Lord of the Rings*, and believe it or not, his time on the set only intensified that.

Getting "under the skin" of a certain elf broadened his couture horizons.

"Before that, I would never have thought to wear something like velvet," said Orlando, "but now something like that works for me. It's just a little larger than life."

Orlando appeared in more and more interviews and even had his own Legolas doll at Burger King!

Before the movie hit theaters, fans were already seeing the chiseled Bloom face in magazines and falling quickly in love. The more people saw him, the more they wanted to know about him.

Even his co-workers lent a hand in fueling the flames of infatuation in Orlando's fans. When *USA Today* asked Peter Jackson to describe each cast member in one word, his word for Orlando was "passionate."

Orlando's fans were learning much about the new object of their desire. They learned that while he spends time in L.A., London is his true love, and he'll always return to it. They learned that Orlando is, as one magazine creatively called him, "the embodiment of the modern hippie," that he doesn't read magazines or watch television, but he does sculpt, and that he lives a vegan lifestyle, avoiding not only meat, but dairy as well. (Although he has since changed that a bit, saying he *will* down the occasional steak.)

But if fans quickly took notice when they saw Orlando in the press, their reaction when the movie finally premiered was *wild*.

When *The Lord of the Rings: The Fellowship of the Ring* hit theaters on December 19, 2001, it became clear that the executives at New Line Cinema could breathe easy. The film was an unparalleled success. Fans loved it. Critics raved. And the enormous cost of the film's production, promotion, and marketing was more than paid for in the first two weeks! To date, the first *Lord of the Rings* film alone has made over $867 million at the box office, not counting DVD sales!

Almost overnight, anyone in the cast who wasn't already a star became one. And Orlando was more in demand than he had ever dreamed.

Virtually overnight, fan mail poured in, Web sites rose up, and the "cult" of Orlando Bloom was officially on its way. For this serious actor who wanted nothing more than to be the best at his craft, life would never be the same.

CHAPTER EIGHT
BIRTH OF A STAR

After months of publicity madness, Orlando needed a break.

The exhausting press for *The Fellowship of the Ring* had ended in Australia just before the film's release, so Orlando and several of his friends decided to go to India for Christmas to chill out and escape what it now seemed would be the complete madness generated by the film's premiere.

Unfortunately, because of the media hype *before* the movie's opening, Orlando had to check into hotels under an assumed name. (One alias he liked to use was Travis Bickle, Robert De Niro's character in the legendary Martin Scorsese film *Taxi Driver*.)

Orlando had a great holiday with his friends, but by the time he returned to Los Angeles in January, the Orlando Bloom popularity explosion was off and running. By mid-January, his name was one of the most searched-for terms on the Internet and *the* most searched for term associated with the film other than the film title itself. A Google.com search for his name in January 2002 uncovered over 29,000 hits.

The oddest thing about this was that Orlando's part in *The Fellowship of the Ring* was minor. In the film, he shoots some arrows and keeps watch, calling the group's attention to invaders a few times. But his serious exchanges are minimal. It turns out that fans didn't need an in-depth portrait of Orlando to find themselves hooked. As the saying goes, just one look was all it took.

And to improve Orlando's lot even further, *Black Hawk Down* premiered in January as well!

Black Hawk Down was wonderfully reviewed (the director, Ridley Scott, was ultimately nominated for an Oscar), and it was a very different film than *Lord of the Rings.*

Again, Orlando wasn't in the movie that long. But his short time on-screen was enough to satisfy the growing ranks of Orlando fanatics. He looked much more babyish than in *Lord of the Rings.* His regal blond wig was replaced by the Army buzz cut, and he spoke with a southern twang, but it was another side of Orlando, and fans now had two chances to be enthralled by him.

Perhaps not surprisingly, Orlando found that being the new heartthrob wasn't always easy to take. Magazines called him the new Leonardo (as in DiCaprio), and he was often uncomfortable with the attention. If fans knew he was appearing somewhere, a mob would show up to scream his name. Orlando never wanted to bask in the glow of people's adulation. At heart, he was a kind and humble guy who wasn't about seeking attention and praise. He merely wanted to act, do good work, and be respected for that work.

In addition to learning how to deal with the fans, he now also had to remind the people who knew and loved him, his friends and family, that he was still the same, lovable Orlando.

"It's been an adjustment for my mates at home," he said, "because the more publicity you do and the more your face is in magazines or on TV, the harder it is. When your friends read about you more than they get to see you, then you have to keep reassuring people that you aren't changing."

Orlando was also freaked out by all the incredibly detailed Web sites dedicated to him. Orlando, after all, was something of a technophobe. He knew very little about the Internet. (Even at this point, he doesn't have an e-mail address.) His mother wanted him to start an official Web page, but he had little desire to do so. Internet attention simply seemed weird to him.

"That really freaks me out," he said about the Web sites. "That many people taking interest is scary. The Internet is a scary thing."

Orlando wasn't generally thrilled with being looked at as a sex symbol. It's not that he didn't love his fans, of course. It's just that as hard as he'd worked to become a serious actor, he was concerned that the attention paid to his striking looks would distract people from his acting.

Interviewers have noted that Orlando shrinks a bit when the issue of being a sex symbol comes up. Even so, he is gracious about it. He has said that he always appreciates the compliment but that being a sex symbol or teen idol is "a secondary thing to me." Orlando's main focus is on "choosing roles that affect me, that challenge me personally."

At this point, however, the transition to stardom was a bit easier than it might have been. For the most part he was still able to walk down the street virtually undisturbed. That's because he looks very different in real life than he did as Legolas. His hair is dark, where Legolas's was blond, and his eyes are deep brown, as opposed to Legolas's liquid blue. And in *Black Hawk Down*, he had a crew cut. So, while fans were in love with Orlando, most still didn't have the clearest picture of what he *really* looked like.

By late January and early February, Orlando's stardom was becoming more official by the day. The *London Times* proclaimed him a future style icon for British men, calling him "gorgeous, undeniably well-dressed, and one of the future's biggest stars." *Elle* magazine cited him as "one to look out for in 2002." E! Entertainment Television named him one of the "Sizzlin' 16 of 2002," a list that in previous years included Jennifer Lopez, Hilary Swank, Vin Diesel, Ben Affleck, and Matt Damon. *Teen People* called him one of the "25 Hottest Stars Under 25," and *YM* proclaimed him one of the "20 Hottest Guys" of the year.

But not all the press focused on his looks. *Movieline,* an American movie magazine, called Orlando's portrayal of Legolas one of the "Ten Best Performances by Young Actors in 2001," adding that Peter Jackson's hiring of Orlando was his "gutsiest choice." And *Empire* magazine, a major British entertainment publication that hosts a major annual awards show called "The Empire Awards," nominated Orlando for Best Debut Performance.

The actual Empire Awards ceremony was a wonderful night of glamour for Orlando and his first taste of real show biz adulation. Readers of *Empire* magazine voted for Orlando in overwhelming numbers. He beat out surfing pals Billy Boyd and Dominic Monaghan (and his future *Pirates of the Caribbean* co-star Keira Knightley) to win the Best Debut award. He gave a poignant and funny acceptance speech, thanking Peter Jackson and his wife, Fran, for seeing some "pointy-eared quality in me."

Kate Winslet, who also won an award that night for Best British Actress for the film *Enigma*, even made a point of mentioning in her acceptance speech that she found Orlando's performance "brilliant!"

To make the night even more special, Elijah Wood won for Best Actor and *The Lord of the Rings* won for Best Picture.

Soon after, Orlando was hired to shoot a commercial for the Gap. But this wasn't just any commercial. In an effort to create a series of groundbreaking ads for its summer khakis, the Gap hired several Academy Award–winning filmmakers, including Cameron Crowe and the Coen brothers, to create 30-second, black-and-white commercials. Orlando was hired to work with Cameron Crowe, the director of such films as *Almost Famous, Say Anything,* and *Jerry Maguire.* In their 30-second spot, titled "Denim Invasion," Orlando and actress Kate Beckinsale (*Pearl Harbor*) play a couple who are out for a summer stroll when they slowly notice they're being followed by admirers. By the spot's end, the couple is actually being chased down the street by a crowd.

Once the commercial aired, it seemed as if everything Orlando touched truly turned to gold. The spot was quickly regarded as one of the most entertaining on television. *TV Guide* featured the commercial on its "Cheers and Jeers" page (as a Cheer, of course), calling it "the most charming 30 seconds on TV." One newspaper even proclaimed it the best commercial on television because of the "look of joyous surprise" on the faces of Orlando and Kate when they are suddenly followed by the crowd.

Orlando was now so hot that virtually everything he did provoked a rumor of some kind. Soon after the Gap commercial aired, some papers ran pictures of Orlando and Kate from the taping, hinting that they were now a couple! Untrue, as Orlando was still officially "married to his work."

After sorting through many different offers, Orlando had finally decided on his next major project. And wouldn't you know, he was now headed back down to the Southern Hemisphere, not far from the area in which he made *The Lord of the Rings.*

He was making his next major movie in Australia.

CHAPTER NINE
ORLANDO THE OUTLAW

Until now, Orlando had done an incredible job of taking on roles that were both heroic and considerably more important than average.

With *The Lord of the Rings*, a virtual cult of fans awaited the production, ready to pounce if every line and character wasn't perfect. In *Black Hawk Down*, he played a real soldier involved in a conflict where 18 American soldiers lost their lives. Had that film not been respectful and accurate, it would have upset many people for even stronger reasons.

So while still in his twenties, Orlando had already chosen two roles that had a responsibility not only to the film itself, but to history.

With his next major role, this pattern would continue.

Ned Kelly was a Robin Hood–type outlaw who lived in Australia in the late 1800s. He and his gang, including his brother Dan and his friends Joe Byrne and Steve Hart, robbed banks and ran from the law before being caught and executed while still in their twenties. The gang members were colorful figures who wore cast-iron buckets on their heads during holdups to conceal their identities.

But Ned Kelly wasn't just your average eccentric outlaw. He was one of the most heroic and worshiped figures in Australian history. That's because Kelly was a legend, and a symbol of Australia's oppressed poor people.

Like many in Australia during those times, the Kelly family were Irish immigrants. Ned, who was born in Australia, was sent to prison at 16 for a crime that, legend has it, he didn't commit. When he got out a few years later, a police officer assaulted his sister. When Ned and his mother tried to defend their family, Ned's mother was thrown in prison, and Ned and his brother began a life on the run. From the beginning, Ned Kelly was seen as a symbol of the toughness and independence of the Australian people.

The Kelly Gang began stealing to support themselves but soon became the most notorious outlaws of their time.

No Australian has been written about and filmed more than Ned Kelly. The first feature-length movie *ever*, in fact, was the 1906 *The Story of the Kelly Gang*, and a 1970 film version of the story, also titled *Ned Kelly*, starred Rolling Stone Mick Jagger.

When Orlando first heard that a movie was being made of Ned Kelly's life, however, he knew none of this.

Orlando met with the film's director, Gregor Jordan, in Los Angeles. Gregor wanted Orlando to play Joe Byrne, Ned Kelly's right-hand man. In addition to telling him all about the rich history of the Kelly Gang, Gregor told Orlando that the project would return him to the Australian continent and that much of his part would involve shooting guns and riding horses throughout the Australian countryside.

At one point, the film even has a scene where the four gang members cover themselves in armor, grab their Colt .32s, and head right into a firefight with over 200 police officers!

But while Orlando was excited by the action, Gregor also explained that the violence had a larger purpose. "They felt they were persecuted unjustly," explains Orlando, "so it sounded like something to be involved in. Camaraderie, loyalty, friendship, and standing up for what you believe in are all themes I can relate to."

Equally exciting was the opportunity to work with yet another amazing cast. The hot Australian actor Heath Ledger was slated to play Ned Kelly. Oscar winner Geoffrey Rush would play the lawman charged with hunting them down. And Australian actresses Naomi Watts and Rachel Griffiths would also be in the film.

Orlando quickly agreed to take the part of Joe Byrne.

"It was so rewarding playing a character who was a hero in real life to so many Australians," said Orlando. "It was gratifying to discover the historical details and to explore the impact of the Kelly Gang on the entire nation. It really moved me."

In addition to the rich history involved in the story, the wonderful location, and the great cast, the character of Byrne himself was a great departure for Orlando—heroic, perhaps, but in a very different way than Legolas or a U.S. Army Ranger.

Byrne was certainly a danger-loving outlaw, but he was much more than that. He was the intelligent, thoughtful outlaw of the Kelly Gang. He was well educated, speaking several languages, including Cantonese. He was known as a glamorous gangster, being incredibly stylish for his day, and he had a charming way with the ladies.

While the Kelly Gang was notorious for wearing homemade armor to protect themselves during gunfights, Joe Byrne's fashion sense went way beyond metal and iron. He even wore high-heeled boots that would become his trademark! So in a sense, Orlando got to play a smooth-talking Casanova, a fashion maven, and an outlaw—all in one role!

"The members of the gang were criminals, but my character is also a real ladies' man, so I'm going to have to kiss several actresses in the film. What a great job!" Orlando says with a laugh.

On a more serious note, the personal path Joe Byrne traveled over the course of the film was a significant and challenging one for Orlando.

"Joe's journey is really incredible," he explains. "I had to keep reminding myself that he was only 21 when he died, because he fit a lot into so short and spectacular a life. Joe's the dark horse, the calm to Ned's rage," says Orlando. "He really is that lukewarm water between the fire and ice of this story. And one thing's for sure, he would go to hell and back for Ned—and does."

Joe Byrne allowed Orlando to take the heroic themes he had built so far in his career and expand on them, give them more depth. Legolas was pure, quiet strength, and Private Blackburn, as Orlando played him, was a naive southern boy thrown into incredible circumstances. Joe Byrne was perhaps the most complex character Orlando had played so far, walking a sometimes hard-to-define line between good and evil. He was a criminal but a patriot, both a charmer and a killer. As an actor always looking to broaden his horizons, this was a great opportunity for Orlando.

In the time leading up to the filming, Orlando did everything he could to get as deep into Joe's psyche as possible, to really learn what made this complicated man tick. He read lots of books about the Kelly Gang, saw films, and visited locations. But occasionally, as he had with Legolas, he delved so deeply into the complicated Joe Byrne psyche that he had to pull himself back.

For example, Heath Ledger had obtained a photo of Ned Kelly that he looked at every day because it really made him feel like he knew the character. So Orlando decided to follow his lead and seek out a picture of Joe Byrne. The only one he found, though, was of Joe after he had been hanged, a photo where Joe was what Orlando described as "twisted and bloody."

The picture was available through an auction, and Orlando had planned to bid on it. But on the morning of the auction, he changed his mind. That's because the night before, he had a very disturbed sleep. Orlando tossed and turned, having awful dreams.

He soon realized that he needed to "be immersed in Joe Byrne the man," not the guy hanging dead in the photo. "I believe in connections," said Orlando, "and something told me that photo was the wrong energy. I decided that I didn't need a picture of a dead man in my life."

That wasn't the only night Orlando felt Joe Byrne's presence. Throughout the shoot, Orlando and his cast mates felt the ghosts of the Kelly Gang close by. "There were nights I had real trouble sleeping, and I blamed Joe," said Orlando. "See, for all his composure under fire, there was a real twistedness to his soul."

While Orlando was able to explore the depth of his character, he was also able to have fun on a more superficial level. Joe Byrne spoke in a rich

Irish brogue—a far cry from Orlando's native British tongue.

Orlando enjoyed talking in the Irish accent so much that he kept it going while off the set. He would chat up patrons in local pubs and stores, talking as if he was the reincarnation of good ol' Joe Byrne himself. He was so immersed in his character that he spoke in the Irish accent throughout his entire Australian stay—and then even fell back on it occasionally for a laugh once he returned to Los Angeles!

The shoot began on April 29, 2002, and from the very beginning the weight of history was inescapable for the cast. They shot much of the film near the actual locations where the events actually took place. The history of the Kelly Gang literally surrounded them! The apartment that Heath Ledger stayed in, for example, overlooked the exact spot where Ned Kelly had been hanged.

And not only did their locations remind them how important this story was to the people of Australia, but so did the Australians themselves. When the first pictures of Heath made up as Ned Kelly were released to the press, every paper in Australia ran them—some even on the front page!

Australians weren't merely relying on the

papers to bring them reports, either—they were going down to the shoot to see for themselves. Throughout the production, the set was mobbed by as many as 5,000 people at once. Some would even approach the cast or crew, look them straight in the eye, and say, "Don't mess this up!"

They needn't have worried. The cast members were mostly Australian, so they understood the importance of the Kelly legend to the Australian people. "Ned has been haunting a lot of young Australian males for over a century now," said Heath. "I know he haunted me." And even those who weren't Australian—like Orlando—never failed to grasp the responsibility placed at their feet.

Late in the filming, a story hit the press that the studio was unhappy with the footage because their two hunky co-stars, Heath and Orlando, had grown big, bushy beards. The studio was reportedly worried that adoring fans wouldn't want to see those gorgeous faces covered by big piles of hair. But the cast—Heath in particular—wanted the film to be as historically accurate as possible and wanted the beards to stay. As it happened, it would have been too late in the filming to reshoot all the beard scenes anyway. When asked about it, the studios denied that they had a problem with the beards. The beards stayed in the picture.

While Orlando was shooting *Ned Kelly,* some of his old mates were getting together close by. Peter Jackson brought some of the *Lord of the Rings* cast back to New Zealand for some minor reshoots. Unfortunately, Orlando couldn't participate because he had the beard, and he couldn't exactly be a dashing elf with a big face full of fuzz. But that didn't mean he couldn't hop across the island during a weekend off and spend some time with his old friends!

Orlando had a dinner party with Viggo and some of the others, and they had a wild night out on the town, visiting their old haunts and reliving the camaraderie they had so enjoyed during filming.

While Orlando was in Australia, his buzz was growing throughout the world— especially back in the States. MTV announced the nominations for the MTV Movie Awards in April 2002, and *The Lord of the Rings* led the pack with six nominations. Orlando received the music channel's nod for Best Male Breakthrough Performance, pitting him against DMX, Colin Hanks, Daniel Radcliffe, and Paul Walker.

The awards ceremony was held in June.

Orlando was still in Australia when he was notified that he had *won!* He gave his acceptance speech holding his moon man via satellite from down under.

Once Orlando got the award, cast mates began asking about his future projects. Orlando proudly told them that he already had his next project nailed down. It was slated to be both his first starring role *and* his first comedy.

In the low-budget British film *The Calcium Kid*, Orlando was set to play a milkman and amateur boxer who winds up unexpectedly fighting the world champion.

Orlando agreed to film *The Calcium Kid* for several reasons. First, as was important for all his roles, *The Calcium Kid* would present him with new challenges, both physically and professionally. He'd need to train as a boxer and would also gain his first comedy experience on film.

He also agreed to the film because the director, Alex De Rakoff, was a friend of his. Alex was an experienced music video director who had worked with Ice-T, N-Trance, and others, but this would be his feature film debut. Orlando agreed to the film, proud to help his friends when they needed him.

But *Ned Kelly* cast mate Geoffrey Rush began

talking to Orlando about a project he would be filming in the near future—a movie from Disney. He kept urging Orlando to read the script. The film Geoffrey Rush referred to was *Pirates of the Caribbean: The Curse of the Black Pearl.*

Orlando had first heard about *Pirates* from its producer, Jerry Bruckheimer—the same man who produced *Black Hawk Down.* Back when Orlando and Bruckheimer were in Japan promoting *Black Hawk Down,* the director told Orlando that Disney was doing a movie based on its *Pirates of the Caribbean* ride. Now Geoffrey thought Orlando should read for the part of Will Turner, a young man who joins with a crazy pirate captain to rescue the kidnapped daughter of an influential governor. Geoffrey was going to be playing the girl's kidnapper, the villainous Captain Barbossa.

Orlando didn't want to read the script at first. *The Calcium Kid* and *Pirates of the Caribbean* were scheduled to film around the same time. He didn't want to get excited about *Pirates* if he wouldn't be able to participate. And while it certainly would be a bigger film than *Calcium,* he had made a commitment to a friend, and Orlando wasn't the type of person to let a friend down.

"I didn't want to do the movie at first," said

Orlando. "I thought, what should I do with an American blockbuster? Besides, I was shooting an independent comedy [*The Calcium Kid*] and didn't have time."

Jerry Bruckheimer sent him the *Pirates* script, and Orlando allowed it to sit in a pile. But then Bruckheimer passed on some other news that caused Orlando to reconsider.

The crazy pirate captain was to be played by none other than Johnny Depp, one of Orlando's biggest inspirations and role models. If Orlando got the part, he'd be working closely with someone he'd admired for years!

Orlando read the script immediately, and the more he read, the more it became apparent that Will Turner would be incredibly exciting to play. The film featured pirates out on the open seas, with lots of sword fights and wall-to-wall action. Orlando had loved pretending to be a pirate as a kid. He watched pirate movies on the weekends and imagined himself in the midst of the boat battles, swinging on ropes, conquering the bad guys, and getting the girl at the end. Will Turner was a part Orlando was born to play.

"We really needed somebody who could hold his own as the love interest–Errol Flynn character so the audience wouldn't think Keira was going to end up with Johnny Depp," explained the film's director, Gore Verbinski.

Geoffrey suggested Orlando for the part, and Gore met with Orlando and actress Keira Knightley, who had already been cast as the governor's daughter. As they ate and talked, Gore kept stealing glances at these two hot young stars, who must have looked like the most gorgeous couple on the planet, and thought, "This could work."

So now Orlando wanted the part, and the producer and director wanted Orlando. The only thing that stood in his way was *The Calcium Kid*. But as happened so often with Orlando, things worked themselves out.

The producers of *The Calcium Kid* and *Pirates of the Caribbean* were able to fix their scheduling problems. Orlando would film *The Calcium Kid* for six weeks in England and then fly out to Los Angeles the next day to join the set of *Pirates*.

The Calcium Kid was a mockumentary, not unlike the movies *Best in Show* or *This Is Spinal Tap*. Orlando's character, Jimmy, is a real "working man's hero," according to Orlando, who drinks so much milk that his bones become remarkably strong. During a sparring match, the leading

British contender to the title breaks his hand on Jimmy's super-powerful jaw. When the boxing promoters see this, they arrange for the extremely-unqualified Jimmy to fight the champion on only six days' notice.

Part of the joke of the role is that despite his solid bones, Jimmy isn't really a good boxer. While this made for some interesting comedy, Orlando found boxing to be quite a challenge.

First he had to undergo boxing training. Since his schedule was so tight, he did his boxing training in Australia while on the *Ned Kelly* set. Then once he got to London, he spent a few weeks working out, making himself really buff. (Yes, that's right. *The Calcium Kid* features a very buff Orlando spending lots of his time in the boxing ring—without a shirt!)

But not only did Orlando have to learn boxing; he had to play a *bad* boxer, which he insists was much harder than it might sound. "You watch two huge guys slugging it out and you're like, 'Well, okay,'" said Orlando. "But when you actually stand in the ring and try to punch for three minutes, it's exhausting."

After several highly acclaimed blockbusters featuring megastars, some wondered why Orlando would make such a small and different film. But as he had proved time and again, Orlando was wise beyond his years when it came to making career decisions. At this point, he was ready for a leading role. But at the same time, he wanted the situation to be something he could have fun with and not stress out about.

"I wanted my first lead to be in a film that wouldn't require me to be hugely responsible for a budget of a hundred million dollars," Orlando said. "I wanted to do something light and show another side of myself. I make a fool of myself. I relished the chance."

Overall, the six-week *Calcium Kid* shoot turned out to be the most creatively rewarding experience of Orlando's career. After all the fantasy, he welcomed the chance to do a straightforward, current, simple picture. It was also his first chance to really carry a movie. He therefore had "loads of dialogue, exercising muscles that had been lying dormant," according to Orlando.

"Because it was a small movie, we had six weeks to film it, we had a lot to get through, and we just had to keep moving. It was a good process for me," said Orlando.

He later told an interviewer during a press trip

for *Pirates* that while he loved all the films he's shot, *The Calcium Kid* is the one he hopes all his fans go see. "I can only hope the people who write me thousands of letters will go see this," he said. "I feel proud of what it meant for me."

But that's not to say that Orlando hasn't appreciated each and every opportunity he's had on-screen. Orlando never forgets how lucky he has been to have such a great variety of roles, each one teaching him new things about acting and life in the process. Around the time of *The Calcium Kid*, he said to a friend, "Man, I've been an elf, a soldier boy, a boxer, a pirate, and an outlaw. I really am living every boy's dream!"

With his next film, that wonderful dream was about to continue, full steam ahead.

For *Pirates of the Caribbean*, Orlando was off to another exotic location—this time, as the name indicates, the beautiful sun-drenched Caribbean.

The movie was a considerable step up for Orlando since it was his biggest part in a major production yet. And as Orlando so loved, he'd get to play great action scenes, with even more intricate sword fighting than he enjoyed in *Lord of the Rings*.

But for Orlando, the most important and exciting aspect of the filming, by far, was working with Johnny Depp.

Johnny Depp began his career on a Fox television show called *21 Jump Street*. He was a teen idol at the time, not unlike Orlando now. Girls adored him, and any serious critic dismissed him as just good-looking fluff, a luscious piece of eye candy that was empty at the center.

But Johnny did something that at first surprised

many onlookers. He left the show, subsequently turning away the traditional "hot guy" roles that many would have expected him to take. Instead he played quirkier parts in small but well-written films like *Edward Scissorhands,* where his character was made to look unattractive—to the point of being grotesque. The reaction of those in Hollywood began as disbelief but quickly changed to admiration. People soon realized exactly what Depp wanted them to—that underneath those glimmering good looks lays a wealth of intelligence and acting talent.

There are so many ways that Johnny Depp's career could have gone differently, so many films that might have paid him more money and brought him more admiration as a Hollywood heartthrob. But those roles wouldn't have had the kind of quality he desired.

Since leaving *21 Jump Street,* Johnny Depp has solidified his place in Hollywood as one of our finest actors, someone who can always be counted on to play interesting parts in unique films and never to insult his audience.

It isn't difficult, therefore, to understand why Johnny Depp is one of Orlando's idols. Depp shunned style for substance, just as Orlando sought to do now.

"Johnny's funny," says Orlando. "He said to me, 'I've made a career out of making movies that are failures.'

"Johnny has always been some kind of idol for me," Orlando continues, "someone who was judged by his looks to be the leading man and despite that stayed true to himself."

The issue of how to handle being admired for his looks is something Orlando thinks about quite a bit. While he certainly appreciates the fans and is grateful for the attention, he does worry that he may get sucked into making bad choices. Looking at Johnny Depp, Orlando realized that there was a certain rite of passage someone in his position needed to go through—just as Johnny did with *21 Jump Street*.

"This heartthrob thing was created around him," said Orlando, "but now he's able to do whatever he likes, and people love to work with him. I'm hoping that I'll get the same opportunity."

To Orlando's joy, he and Depp hit it off fantastically on the set of *Pirates*. Orlando described it as an instant click—the second they met, they liked each other immensely.

Orlando enjoyed working with Johnny on two levels. On the set, Orlando played the straight man to Johnny's crazy pirate. He got to watch Johnny work up close, really analyze what he did, and learn from the acting choices he made. Then off the set he got to not only pal around with his idol, but also talk to him about how to handle fame. It was then that Johnny gave Orlando some of the best career advice that Orlando would ever receive. "Never make a decision for or against a movie because of the money!" Johnny told him. Orlando listened closely and "engraved" that piece of advice in his mind.

In *Pirates of the Caribbean*, Orlando's character, the blacksmith Will Turner, was something of a return to Legolas—very straitlaced, noble, and heroic. Will falls in love with the governor's daughter, Elizabeth Swann, who is played by Keira Knightley. When Elizabeth is kidnapped, Will has to join forces with Johnny Depp's character, the somewhat demented pirate Captain Jack Sparrow.

Will has a tough time handling the just-south-of-insane Sparrow but has to work with him to rescue his true love. The differences in their characters made for a lot of funny scenes as these two very different creatures try to figure out how to deal with each other. As the movie evolves, Will learns more and more about unleashing his own "inner pirate."

To prepare for the film, Orlando needed to learn sword fighting at a deeper level. In *Lord of the Rings*, his main physical focus had been bow and arrow. For *Pirates*, he'd have to start his training from scratch.

Once again, Orlando got to work with the best, Bob Anderson, whom he worked with on *Lord of the Rings*.

For Orlando, part of the challenge of being Will Turner was remembering that *he* was playing the straight man. While filming some earlier scenes, the director, Gore Verbinski, had to continually remind Orlando that he wasn't supposed to be "cool" just yet.

"I had to say to him, 'Listen, you're still a dork!'" said Gore. "And he'd go, 'Oh yeah, yeah, yeah! Right! I'm still a dork! Got it!'"

Apparently it took every ounce of self-control Orlando could muster to not act as cool as possible around his idol.

On set, Orlando learned that one of the most amazing things about acting with Johnny was the immense amount of characterization Johnny brought to his role. In the script, Captain Jack

Sparrow wasn't nearly as crazy as he eventually appears on film. Johnny took the character from the page and re-formed him completely. It was an inspiring lesson for Orlando.

"When you read the script, Johnny's character didn't read like that," said Orlando. "Jack Sparrow read like a bit of a rogue, but a sort of straight rogue. What Johnny did was create this incredible kind of sea-legged, drunken, Keith Richards number. He created that and that's what he does so well."

This was a stroke of luck for Orlando because had Johnny played Jack Sparrow in a more conventional manner, it would have been boring for Orlando to be just as straitlaced. With Johnny taking the wacky angle, that left the door wide open for Orlando to play the typical romantic lead—the hero.

But Orlando didn't just emphasize the traditional aspects of Will Turner. Ever the shrewd actor, he found a way for himself to join in with Johnny's insanity. During a flight to the Caribbean, Orlando was talking with Jerry Bruckheimer and Johnny and said, "I really want to be doing what Johnny is doing! Maybe I could do an impression of him." Johnny and Jerry both thought it was a great idea, and Jerry said, "Yeah, man, we'll write that in!'"

Just like that, Orlando had himself a cool new scene to play—and way to pay homage to his role model, Johnny!

In fact, Orlando was so inspired by Johnny on the set of *Pirates* that he did something actors rarely do—he suggested fewer close-ups of himself and more shots of him and the mad pirate *together* on-screen.

"It was like *The Odd Couple* because of what Johnny was doing," said Orlando. "It was just great to work with him. I love sharing the screen with the guy." And as it happened, Orlando got to do just that for the whole movie, something that never stopped freaking him out.

Will Turner stared at Jack Sparrow in just about every scene of the movie, wondering, "What the heck is this weirdo doing?" But in real life, Orlando was looking at Johnny and thinking, "This is so cool! I can't believe I'm doing this!"

Despite how much acclaim Johnny Depp would receive for the role of Jack Sparrow—including an eventual Oscar nomination for Best Actor—Orlando was also noticed for his portrayal. Many even compared him to Errol Flynn, the old-time actor who was generally known as the best pirate actor in Hollywood.

To excel at the character, Orlando immersed himself in the pirate world, reading books on the subject and watching old Errol Flynn movies like *Captain Blood* and *The Master of Ballantrae*.

While his sword-fighting lessons had brought Orlando's skills to a whole new level, the fact that he had worked with swords on *Lord of the Rings* certainly helped.

Orlando remarked that once he started his classes with Bob, it was like riding a bike—you remember the basics even if you haven't done it for a while. He called it a "muscle memory."

But even though Orlando did well, there were certainly some nicks and cuts along the way. After all, it wouldn't be Orlando if there weren't a few injuries, right?

During one scene that took place in a blacksmith's shop, Johnny had to throw hammers at Orlando, and a few of them hit Orlando a bit harder then he might have liked. Even after the shoot was completed, Orlando still had the bruises!

"My sword fight with Johnny was an intimidating routine," admits Orlando. "When the stunt guys showed us our moves, we were like, 'Are you crazy? You expect us to do that?'"

That scene was originally scheduled for early in the shoot, but since Orlando was coming straight from the set of *The Calcium Kid*, he wanted more time to work on his skills and really be prepared. So the scene was rescheduled for later.

The rescheduling also helped in that it allowed Johnny and Orlando to develop a friendship and bond a bit before shooting the scene.

"In the end it was great fun," said Orlando. "I'd developed a great relationship with Johnny, and in fact a couple of things didn't make it into the final movie. Johnny was coming up with things like butt slaps, he was smacking my bum with his sword, but it didn't make it into the film because unfortunately it wasn't where we could go with the characters at that point."

The sword-fighting scene was very hard work, which of course Orlando was well used to by now. The hardest part, it turned out, was the dust that surrounded them on the set.

There was so much dust on the floor for that scene that it kept kicking up and getting into everyone's noses. "Everyone would come out blowing their noses. It was truly filthy," Orlando said. "I know everyone says actors moan too much, but it's not very reassuring for an actor when they walk on set and they have to act, and everyone else in the crew is wearing a mask!"

Add to those challenges the fact that much of the movie was actually shot out at sea—so the cast had to execute many of their hard physical moves with waves rocking them all around the ship!

"We'd be on a boat 20 miles out at sea," said Orlando, "and sometimes the swirls would get really big, but you couldn't get off it!" As a result, much of the cast and crew took seasickness tablets to help them deal with the rocking. Orlando never got seasick, although he did say that certain cast and crew members spent some time hanging over the rail.

But while Johnny and Orlando talked about the hard physical work, the stunts, and the risky maneuvers that actors often do on set, Orlando learned yet another important lesson—this one, perhaps, the lesson he needed most.

Johnny Depp taught Orlando that the physical risk doesn't always need to be his and that he didn't need to leave every film shoot with broken bones.

That, after all, is what stunt doubles are for.

"Johnny said to me, 'Look, the stunt guys are paid to do that, and they're really good at it, so let them do it,'" said Orlando. "'Don't kill yourself for it. You've got a whole career ahead of you.'"

In the midst of all the high-seas high jinks, there was plenty of opportunity for the cast to have fun off the set as well. The shoot took place on the island of St. Vincent, in the Virgin Islands, and at one point, Johnny, Orlando, and producer Jerry Bruckheimer were flown on a private plane to meet the Prime Minister of St. Vincent.

By the time they got there, they were all in a bit of a giddy mood.

"The Prime Minister was there to meet us," said Orlando, "and he goes, 'Hey, man, very pleased to introduce you to St. Vincent.'"

Johnny got off the plane, saw the prime minister waiting for them, and immediately threw his arms around the man and started kissing him!

That's the way it was on the set—the cast was always joking, always having fun.

But Orlando also had his nervous moments, like when he had to kiss his co-star, Keira Knightley, on-screen. Orlando still wasn't completely comfortable with kissing scenes, and this particular kiss would come with more pressure than most since it was in close-up—and it was the sweeping romantic conclusion to the film!

While Keira said that kissing Orlando came naturally, Orlando was unsure about certain . . . mechanics.

"You're sort of like—to tongue or not to tongue? Should it be real or shouldn't it?!" said Orlando, who added, "I like to think I'm romantic!"

When asked about Keira, Orlando said that placed in that circumstance, the urge to fall in love with his comely co-star was strong.

"She's got a boyfriend, damn it!" said Orlando. "She's in love with him, he was around the set the whole time, and I couldn't compete! I was heart-broken!"

Of course, Keira was just was taken with her handsome co-star, who she admiringly calls "a one-man boy band."

"He's fancyable," says Keira, using the British slang term for being totally hot. "I think he's got that androgynous sort of boyish look—a totally attractive boyish look. He's sort of unthreatening to teenage girls, I suppose. I mean, gorgeous. And he's fun to kiss. He was lovely to kiss."

Not only was Orlando a good kisser, but he was

a complete gentleman about it. "He was very professional, but we always had a giggle," says Keira. "And he was kind enough to make sure he had mints and mouthwash beforehand."

So from Keira's perspective, Orlando had no worries about the quality of his kisses. Keira, on the other hand, had some concerns about facing the wrath of Orlando's jealous fans.

"We were filming our kiss, and some woman brought her daughters to the set," Keira recalls. "I thought I was going to be lynched by a little blond mob."

In the end, *Pirates* was just the latest in Orlando's string of incredibly rewarding experiences. To make the moment even sweeter, the second *Lord of the Rings* movie, *The Lord of the Rings: The Two Towers*, premiered while *Pirates* was filming.

The second *Rings* film was darker and more intense than the first, and Orlando was featured much more prominently. He had more dialogue and more on-screen action.

The Two Towers really allowed Orlando time to shine. In one battle scene, he slid down a staircase on a shield, firing arrows the whole time. Then once he hit the bottom, he kicked the shield into an opponent, vanquishing him.

As 2003 approached, Orlando continued his streak as one of the hottest young actors in Hollywood. And not surprisingly, more success was on the way.

CHAPTER ELEVEN
A STAR IN BLOOM

Around the beginning of 2003, rumors starting springing up that Orlando was dating *Blue Crush* actress Kate Bosworth.

This wasn't the first time rumors had surfaced about Orlando's dating life. The media reported for some time that he had dated actress Christina Ricci. Orlando denied this, saying that the two just happened to be dancing together at a party and had their picture snapped. The media had jumped to conclusions.

But given the level of his current fame, the media pressed the subject harder than ever. While he occasionally used to get asked about girlfriends, now the interest in his personal life was constant. Plus the person he was rumored to be dating was also a celebrity. So, just about every interviewer was now asking Orlando the question—are you and Kate an item?

As it turned out, they were. But good-hearted Orlando remained a gentleman throughout. He was never one to kiss and tell and never actually confirmed that the two were an item until late into the year. The closest he came was admitting to an Australian magazine in April that his girlfriend was blond.

Just because Orlando was famous and had achieved his greatest dreams didn't mean he was going to forget basic human values like courtesy and respect. For if there was one thing Orlando knows well, it's how to treat the girls he dates.

"It's all the little things that count, I suppose," Orlando says. "When I'm in love, that woman is the most important thing in my life. I do everything for her."

Orlando has always had a keen sense of how to make girls swoon, but now he also had the opportunity to learn how to be in love when his career played such a major part in his life.

He had dated several women since he and his *Lord of the Rings* girlfriend broke up and had put as much effort into it as humanly possible. (Orlando flew all the way to the Middle Eastern nation of Dubai to be with one girl, and another time, he had fallen in love with someone from Ireland and sent her plane tickets to come visit him!) For while Orlando is, in so many ways, a man of action, he is also a hopeless romantic who cherishes being in love.

"When you start falling for somebody and you can't stop thinking about when you're going to see them again, I love that," Orlando admits.

So he never went into detail about his relationship with Kate Bosworth. But he did finally tell a German magazine in September that Kate was the sweetest girl in the world and that they had been together for "some months" and were very happy.

He mentioned that they rarely got to see each other since both of their careers were doing so well. He also sweetly said that "Kate is perfect for me—we share many of the same interests." (He also mentioned that Kate was a much better surfer than he was—which makes sense since she starred in the surfer film *Blue Crush*.)

So not only was Orlando's career going swimmingly, but his personal life was in a satisfying place as well.

Ned Kelly premiered in Australia in the spring of 2003 to great acclaim, and while the studio threw an outstanding premiere party, Orlando had to miss it because he was still filming *Pirates of the Caribbean.*

Once he was done with *Pirates,* his furious filming pace continued since he was about to jump from one blockbuster to another. But before he did that, he had one piece of unfinished business to take care of—Orlando had to return to New Zealand for one final round of reshoots for *Lord of the Rings.*

While the main filming had been completed over two years ago, the cast had reunited several times for reshoots. With the final film premiering later that year, this would be the very last time they would ever officially get together to work on the film.

Standing on the New Zealand set for the final time, Orlando thought about all he had learned since being cast in the trilogy four years ago, how he'd grown as an actor, and all the things he'd do differently if he were just now starting to film *Lord of the Rings.*

"I've changed so much," said Orlando, "and I thought, 'Oh God, I would have done *that* different now. What was I thinking?' I obviously wasn't. I was so nervous. But it was an opportunity, and I love that character. I tried really hard to get it right, and Pete was amazing and directed me really well, and I feel lucky."

After Orlando did his very last shot as Legolas, the crew gave him the clapboard from the shot (that's the board that someone claps down to mark which scene is being shot) as well as Legolas's bow and arrows and a special Legolas clip reel they had cut together and set to music just for him. It was a sad day for Orlando.

"I said good-bye to Leggy," recalled Orlando, using his nickname for the character. "I boxed up the blond wig and the pointy ears. Very sad, to say good-bye to that. It was really emotional, actually, because it was quite an incredible time in my life, filming *Lord of the Rings*. Such a fantastic group of people, and New Zealand was such an amazing place to work."

But Orlando didn't have a lot of time to sit around being emotional. With *Pirates* done and the production of *The Lord of the Rings* officially out of the way, he would now be paired with yet another actor known for rising above the recognition he received for his looks alone.

The movie *Troy* was to be an epic that would rival even *Pirates* and *Lord of the Rings* for its sheer size and scope. Directed by Wolfgang Petersen

(*The Perfect Storm, Air Force One*), *Troy* is a film version of Homer's classic tale *The Iliad,* which told the story of the Trojan War.

The film would star Brad Pitt as the Greek warrior Achilles and Eric Bana, the actor who played The Hulk (and one of Orlando's *Black Hawk Down* co-stars) as Hector, the Prince of Troy. Hector's parents would be played by veteran actors Peter O'Toole and Julie Christie.

Orlando was cast as Hector's younger brother, Paris, who stole Helen of Troy from her husband, Menelaus, the king of Sparta, and wound up kicking off a 10-year war between Greece and Troy in 1193 B.C.

The part required Orlando to do a lot of research since it was based on extremely well-known literary events. But *The Iliad* can be incredibly hard to read, so Orlando got it on CD and listened to it instead. Orlando has commented that while *The Iliad* was difficult to get through, it really is incredibly rewarding once you do. "It's the story of stories, man," he says. "It is fascinating."

The part of Paris would be an incredible departure for Orlando because for the first time in a major film, he was playing the bad guy.

Normally we think of the villain as a violent, savage character. But the ancient Greek society depicted in *Troy* was warlike, and the men were all warriors. Paris was distinguished by *not* being violent. In a society of fighters, Paris was weak, thoughtless, and completely lacking in nobility.

But he was also a lover—certainly an aspect of the character that Orlando's millions of fans would want to see him play.

"Paris is an antihero," says Orlando, "a character whose actions are fundamentally wrong. He goes against all the ideas of manhood and the male energy of the time. He doesn't even try to be a typical alpha male. He's much more romantic. All the other men go out to fight. He stays at home and makes love. So he falls in love with a woman and creates a war because of his lust. He's just a misguided youth."

Making Paris somewhat likable was a challenge that Orlando took to heart. "He's romantic and dashing and handsome and sort of swans to the ladies," said Orlando. "But he doesn't really think about the consequences of his actions."

For Orlando, the chance to tackle this new type of character was yet another important opportunity to demonstrate his range. He made it his mission to ensure that the character wasn't a thin stereotype of evil, but a character with a heart.

One scene Orlando was very nervous about found his character confronting Helen's father. In that scene, he has been beaten and he is scared. And he does the least heroic possible thing at the end.

"I'm standing in front of the woman I love, my father, my brothers, my entire country, and I run away like a girl," said Orlando. "I mean, how am I going to get away with any dignity?"

The role of Paris is Orlando as no one has seen him. The portrayal is certain to add another layer to the incredible talent he has exhibited to date.

While Paris provided Orlando with perhaps his greatest acting challenge, he once again enjoyed some physicality in this role, including a jump off a 100-foot-high cliff and even more bow-and-arrow work.

This caused Orlando to make funny comments to the press about how he had now learned a great variety of skills from movies—shooting bows and arrows, swordplay, horseback riding—skills that are all *completely useless* in the real world.

Several press people noted that with all these

skills, Orlando could have been one of the world's greatest criminals—in any century but this one!

The filming for *Troy* was set to take place in London and Malta (which meant back to the Caribbean for Orlando), and once again, it was going to be a tremendous effort. The production would use over 1,000 ships and an astounding 75,000 cast members. Orlando told a reporter that he heard it was the largest movie set ever built—even bigger than the one for *Lord of the Rings*.

And, Orlando admitted, it felt bigger. "What was so amazing about *Lord of the Rings* was that because we had been working together for so long, it felt like family. It felt like a small group of people all doing the same thing. Whereas there are so many people on *Troy*, it just felt big straight off the bat."

But by this point, Orlando was unfazed by the size of the production or the incredible fame of the people around him.

"I am getting much more comfortable," Orlando says. "I was doing a scene with Peter O'Toole, and to be standing there not feeling as petrified as I would have been a couple of years ago . . . I wasn't as intimidated."

At one point during the filming of *Troy*, it occurred to Orlando that there he was, working with some of the greatest actors of our generation, and that he was no longer the new kid. He had been through this before, he knew what he was doing, and he knew in his heart that he was a professional who had earned his right to be there, working with legends. It was a proud moment that allowed Orlando to aim even higher since he was confident that the basics were covered.

By the time he began filming *Troy*, Orlando's popularity was significant. Watching Brad Pitt, he learned even more about how to handle an extraordinary level of fame—a level that Brad knew all too well and Orlando was clearly approaching.

When the cast arrived in Malta for the shoot, they went out to dinner the first night. Afterward Brad and Orlando left the restaurant. They were walking down the street together, just chatting, when all of a sudden a flurry of flashbulbs went off in front of them—seemingly from nowhere.

But while Orlando might have freaked if *he* been the object of all the admiration, he quickly realized that the crowd was there for Brad.

"It felt like the whole of Malta was in the street, just screaming and yelling from the rooftops. It was incredible," Orlando said. "He was swamped. He started a small riot. I turned to Brad and was like, 'Aren't you a little worried, mate?' And Brad whispered in my ear, 'Just keep walking. Smile. Shake hands. And just keep walking.'"

Orlando got a glimpse of how one person can become so famous that his everyday life is unmanageable if not approached from a healthy standpoint. And he probably realized that what he saw that day was a glimpse at his own future.

The funny thing is that while Orlando admired how well Brad handled his fame, Brad had similar comments about Orlando. "Aw, he's a gem," Brad said. "He's got that pure enjoyment of it all, of the trip he's on. I always had to make things so important."

Which only goes to prove the saying: the grass is always greener on the other side.

"I can understand why actors like Johnny become recluses," said Orlando. "It was written in a newspaper in England that if you're going on holiday this summer, why not go to Malta because Brad Pitt's filming there and you might bump into him? It's bizarre to see how one person can have that kind of effect on that many people just immediately. It was really scary."

* * *

In June, Disney threw one of the largest movie premiere parties in history for *Pirates of the Caribbean*. Held in California's Disneyland, the bash cost almost $2 million, and it closed the park to the public for the first time in 48 years.

Disney had go-go girls, jugglers, and stilt walkers, all dressed in classic pirate garb. Since the party invitations called for guests to arrive in their "favorite pirate wear," celebs like Daryl Hannah came in full swashbuckling attire!

Producer Jerry Bruckheimer gave a slew of interviews about the project, and his greatest boast was that he had the insight to bring Johnny and Orlando aboard.

In the warm, still air of early evening, 1,500 distinguished guests walked down a 900-foot-long red carpet that was laid out from the Main Street entrance to Frontierland—the longest red carpet in Hollywood history! Celebrity guests and cast members took the distinguished walk of fame, with the loudest, most deafening screams by far coming for Johnny and Orlando.

Then the guests assembled on a series of bleachers to watch the film on a 40-by-90-foot outdoor screen on Tom Sawyer Island. But before they did, they got to say hello to the cast, which floated by them on a motor-powered raft sailing triumphantly down the Rivers of America waterway.

Over the course of the past four amazing years, Orlando had tasted triumph the likes of which he could never have envisioned as a young boy reciting poetry for his fellow citizens of Canterbury. We can only imagine how his mind must have reeled as he strolled down that long red carpet next to his idol, Johnny Depp, and the most successful producer in Hollywood, Jerry Bruckheimer, as much of the crowd screamed not for Depp or Bruckheimer—but for him.

CHAPTER TWELVE
JUST THE BEGINNING

The entire *Lord of the Rings* venture, from the initial casting to the premiere of the final film, *The Return of the King*, might have been one of the longest production-and-release cycles any group of actors has experienced. It was also, however, the most successful, as the trilogy has generated over $2.8 billion to date in box office receipts alone.

The Lord of the Rings: The Return of the King went on to win a record-tying 11 Oscars, including Best Picture—winning every single award it was nominated for at the 2004 Academy Awards.

The premiere party for *The Return of the King* turned out to be the final time that Orlando would get to enjoy all of his great friends in their favorite place.

In early December, as a show of appreciation for all that the films had contributed to New

Zealand, the people of that country threw a massive ticker tape parade for the cast and crew of *Lord of the Rings.*

While Peter Jackson apologetically told the crowd he couldn't show them the film yet because of all the video cameras there, the cast and crew enjoyed the admiration of over 100,000 fans, many of them dressed as their favorite character; many had camped overnight just to get a glimpse of their heroes.

The people of New Zealand were out of their minds with excitement. Just before the parade, an Air New Zealand 747 with the faces of the characters on it flew over the city, and Orlando's mom had the amazing experience of flying into the country in a plane that had her son's picture on the side!

Orlando rode the parade route in one of a series of classic cars, often stopping to get out, greet fans, and sign autographs. He wore a three-year-old, out-of-print "I Love New Zealand" T-shirt that, after he was photographed wearing it at the parade, became a hot, often-requested item.

He and his mates signed autographs and hugged fans for two hours as every balcony and rooftop in sight swarmed with people straining to catch sight of their idols.

Sean Astin summed up the gratitude the *Lord of the Rings* stars all felt when he said, "There is so much darkness and villainy in the world that this city and this country are a beacon of hope—your huge smiles and friendly faces."

For Orlando, the feelings of joy were so intense, that he could only describe it as "the single most amazing time in my life."

Orlando's growing clout in Hollywood allowed him to take several major steps in 2003. For one, he bought his first house, a place in London that he purchased, as he told reporters, just so he had a place to put all his fan mail.

"I've been getting loads of fan mail, really intense amounts of it," he said. "And I always feel these people have put all this time and effort in so you really want to respond to it in some way, and I'm never in one place long enough to do it."

He also took a major step as a Hollywood player when he co-starred in the crime drama *Haven*—a rare contemporary role for him, but more significantly, a film for which he had his first-ever co-producer credit.

Haven, which was shot in the Cayman Islands,

features Bill Paxton and Gabriel Byrne as a pair of seedy businessmen seeking to escape prosecution for tax crimes by fleeing to the Caymans, and Orlando as a young British man led to commit his own crime because of it.

But *Haven* was just a quick break from the period pieces he is now known for. Because around the same time, Orlando signed on to reunite with director Ridley Scott in *Kingdom of Heaven*, yet another epic that takes place in twelfth-century Europe.

Only this time, Orlando won't be one of the leads. He will be *the* lead—and the hero.

Orlando plays Balian, a young peasant blacksmith during the Crusades (yes, *another* blacksmith) who becomes a noble knight, saves his kingdom, and falls in love with the princess of Jerusalem.

Orlando worked furiously to build up 20 pounds of muscle for the film, which began shooting in January 2004. So, if this is even possible, he'll be even hotter in *Kingdom of Heaven* than he's ever been.

While the film co-stars such notable actors as Oscar nominee Liam Neeson and Oscar winner Jeremy Irons, Orlando is the star of this movie, which is expected in theaters in May 2005.

After this, there is more adventurous blacksmithing to come, as Orlando has already signed on to reprise his role of Will Turner for *Pirates of the Caribbean 2*. There will be romance as well when Orlando stars opposite Kirsten Dunst in the contemporary romance *Elizabethtown*, written and directed by Cameron Crowe.

But while Orlando will certainly continue to thrill us all with epic adventures and Hollywood love stories, he also plans to use his star status in Hollywood to pursue smaller projects that mean something to him personally.

One such project is *The Journey Is the Destination*, the true story of a photojournalist named Dan Eldon who was stoned to death during the Somalian conflict of 1993.

Orlando is hoping that by the time he's done filming *Pirates 2*, he'll be in a position to get this film—which is so important to him—made.

Orlando first heard of *The Journey Is the Destination* years before he filmed *Black Hawk Down*—even before he went to acting school!

His sister had bought the book for his mother, and at the time, Orlando thought it was a lad's book and didn't understand why his mum would want it. But Orlando heard more about the book during the *Lord of the Rings* filming, and by the time he'd acquired an agent and manager, he asked them to look into purchasing the rights.

Eventually Dan Eldon's mother approached Orlando about the project directly.

Because of the direction Orlando's career has taken, it's no surprise that he should focus on a project like this. After all, heroism has held a prominent place in Orlando's career, from Legolas's quest to save Middle-Earth through Will Turner saving the woman he loves.

Now Orlando wants to take on a real-life hero—a man who placed himself in harm's way in order to document one of the great injustices of his time. That Orlando should want to bring this man's story to the screen makes complete sense and will surely be a project that will add even greater layers to this already complex, emotional actor.

"It's kind of like I've been on a long journey with it," said Orlando, "so we've got to do it."

With this determination and everything he's accomplished to date, few can doubt that he will. Because while many a pretty face has shone brightly in Hollywood before fading into obscurity, it has never even been hinted that Orlando Bloom might be one of those one-hit wonders.

Ever since Peter Jackson saw the unknown in front of him and thought, "I've got big plans for this talented young man," the most distinguished producers, directors, and actors in film have considered it a pleasure to work beside him.

At this point in his career and his life, with a leading role in an Academy Award–winning movie and five films that have grossed over $100 million dollars each on his resume—with his name at the top of the list for every major casting agent in Hollywood and his face adorning the screen savers of millions of loving fans worldwide—there is no doubt that Orlando, the beautiful daredevil from Canterbury who used to read poetry to his neighbors, has made it.

Orlando Bloom, the hottest actor in Hollywood, is unquestionably here to stay.

FILMOGRAPHY

2005

> *Pirates of the Caribbean 2*—WILL TURNER

> *Elizabethtown*—DREW BAYLOR

> *Kingdom of Heaven*—BALIAN OF IBELIN

2004

> *Haven*—SHY

> *Troy*—PARIS

2003

> *The Lord of the Rings: The Return of the King*
> —LEGOLAS GREENLEAF

> *The Calcium Kid*—JIMMY

Pirates of the Caribbean: The Curse of the Black Pearl—WILL TURNER

Ned Kelly—JOE BYRNE

2002

The Lord of the Rings: The Two Towers—LEGOLAS GREENLEAF

2001

Black Hawk Down—PRIVATE TODD BLACKBURN

The Lord of the Rings: The Fellowship of the Ring—LEGOLAS GREENLEAF

1997

Wilde—RENTBOY